FATHER FLANAGAN
of BOYS TOWN

Also from Boys Town Press

The Mission Continues: Monsignor Nicholas Wegner of Boys Town

The Ongoing Journey

Journey of Faith

Journey of Hope

Journey of Love

Common Sense Parenting

Common Sense Parenting of Toddlers and Preschoolers

Raising Children Without Losing Your Voice and Your Mind (DVD)

Competing with Character

Teaching Social Skills to Youth

There Are No Simple Rules for Dating My Daughter

A Piece of the Puzzle

No Room for Bullies

Practical Tools for Foster Parents

Boundaries: A Guide for Teens

A Good Friend

Who's in the Mirror?

What's Right for Me?

Friend Me!

Dating!

For a Boys Town Press catalog, call **1-800-282-6657**
or visit our website: **BoysTownPress.org**

Boys Town National Hotline®
1-800-448-3000
A crisis, resource and referral number for kids and parents

FATHER FLANAGAN
of BOYS TOWN

A Man of Vision

HUGH REILLY AND KEVIN WARNEKE

Boys Town, Nebraska

Father Flanagan of Boys Town

Published by the Boys Town Press
14100 Crawford St.
Boys Town, Nebraska 68010

Copyright © 2008, Father Flanagan's Boys' Home

ISBN-13: 978-1-889322-99-5
ISBN-10: 1-889322-99-7

The Boys Town Press is the publishing division of Boys Town, a national organization serving children and families.

Publisher's Cataloging in Publication Data

Reilly, Hugh J.

Father Flanagan of Boys Town : a man of vision / Hugh Reilly and Kevin Warneke. -- 1st ed. -- Boys Town, Neb. : Boys Town Press, c2008.

p. ; cm.

ISBN: 978-1-889322-99-5 ; 1-889322-99-7
Includes bibliographical references.

1. Flanagan, Edward Joseph, 1886-1948. 2. Father Flanagan's Boys' Home. 3. Social work--United States--Biography. 4. Problem children--Institutional care--United States--History. I. Warneke, Kevin. II. Title.

HV876.F4 R45 2008
362.745/0924--dc22   0808

Cover portrait by artist Paul Otero

10 9 8 7 6 5 4 3 2

ACKNOWLEDGMENTS

WE OWE A DEBT OF GRATITUDE to so many others for making this book possible. Boys Town's Executive Director, Fr. Steven Boes, along with John Mollison and Barbara Lonnborg were a driving force in making sure that the full and historically accurate story of Father Flanagan's life was told.

Our research on Father Flanagan's childhood in Ireland would have been incomplete without the assistance and guidance of many people. Assumpta Ward, Fidelma Croghan and the staff at Ballymoe's Father Flanagan Centre were gracious hosts and helped direct us to a variety of local sources. Historian John Brady provided essential information on Ballymoe and the surrounding area in the late 1880s. Pat and Ena Collins invited us into their home and took us on a personalized walking tour of the Flanagan homestead which lies on their property.

Fr. Alan Conway of Sligo answered many of our questions and the staff at Summerhill College in Sligo provided us with background information on Father Flanagan's formative school years at their famous institution.

We spent a fascinating afternoon talking with Dr. Eoin O'Sullivan of Trinity College, Dublin, about Father Flanagan's

1946 visit to Ireland and his criticism of Ireland's youth prison system. We would also like to thank the library staffs at the City Libraries in Belfast, Sligo, Dublin, and Waterford. And a special thank you to Terry Flynn of Carrick On Suir, Ireland, who arranged all of our travel and was helpful in a myriad of ways.

We would like to thank the staff at the University of Nebraska-Omaha's Dr. C.C. and Mabel L. Criss Library, the Harry S. Truman Library and Museum, and the Franklin D. Roosevelt Presidential Library and Museum for their assistance with our research in the United States.

Fr. Val Peter, Executive Director Emeritus of Boys Town, Fr. Clifford Stevens, Edwin Novotny and John Melingagio all provided important information and insight on Father Flanagan's life and career.

Finally, we need to thank the staff at Boys Town's Hall of History, especially Mark Daniels and Tom Lynch. This book would not have been written without their unerring guidance and unsurpassed research abilities.

Table of Contents

PROLOGUE: Their Only Hope   1

CHAPTER 1:   The Boy from Ballymoe   9

CHAPTER 2:   Preparing to Do God's Work   23

CHAPTER 3:   Inspired by a Boy Who Needed a Home   35

CHAPTER 4:   Finding a Home   45

CHAPTER 5:   Building a Village for Little Men   63

CHAPTER 6:   Putting Boys Town on the Map   79

CHAPTER 7:   Welcoming Hollywood   101

CHAPTER 8:   America's No. One War Dad   121

CHAPTER 9:   Helping the Children of Defeat   141

CHAPTER 10:   His Work Continues   161

AFTERWORD: By Father Clifford Stevens   175

                Notes   179

Their Only Hope

JUST OUTSIDE OF MERIDIAN, MISSISSIPPI, Thomas Boykin slowed down to pick up two sailors who were hitch-hiking by the side of the road. It was November 13, 1943, and Boykin, a former sheriff, was on his way home to his wife and children. He figured he could spare a little time to help two boys in uniform.

Joseph Leemon was from Alabama and Murice Shimnick from Wisconsin. They were stationed at the Navy Air Station near Foley, Alabama. Boykin didn't know it, but the two nine-teen-year-olds were AWOL and looking for someone to rob.

"We stayed in Mobile a while," Shimnick told police, according to newspaper accounts. "Then we came to Meridian where Joe had an aunt. We planned to rob someone and take his car, but we had no intention of killing a man. Boykin just happened to be the one we picked to rob."[1]

Shimnick and Leemon came from religious backgrounds; one was a Baptist, the other an evangelical. They had been high school honor students. They hadn't been in the service long, but the experience had changed them.

Shortly after Boykin picked them up, Shimnick slugged the former lawman with a blackjack and forced him to stop the car. Leemon drove the car off the road and the young men dragged Boykin into the woods. "He was yelling and we lost our heads and cut his throat," Shimnick said. "Then we got in the car and drove off. Remembering we had forgotten to take the money off him, we came back for it and then headed to Mobile."[2]

Leemon and Shimnick were apprehended some time later in LaGrange, Georgia, and brought back to Mississippi. After a quick trial in county court, they were convicted and sentenced to be executed by electric chair. The Mississippi State Supreme Court upheld the sentence.

Hundreds of miles away, in Boys Town, Nebraska, Father Edward J. Flanagan read about the boys' trial and conviction. Perhaps he thought of some of the boys he had rescued from prison and brought to Boys Town. Maybe he thought about the hundreds of Boys Town citizens who were fighting in Europe and the Pacific. He may have even thought about the three sailors from Boys Town who were killed in the attack on Pearl Harbor. Whatever his reason, on December 13, 1944, he sat down and wrote a letter to Gov. Thomas L. Bailey of Mississippi.

"I am interested in the cases of Murice Shimnick and Joseph Leemon, who are both members of the Lauderdale County Jail at Meridian, Mississippi, and convicted to die on the 29th of December this year," Flanagan wrote. "Both of these young men were excellent boys from Christian families when they joined the Navy.

"…Your honor, I am not one of these sob sister types that feel that a man should not die for a crime that he has committed in the full possession of his senses and perhaps with

2

premeditation. I think the world is much better off by such men being taken out of it, for they have proven themselves to be unfit and unworthy members of society. I do think, however, your Honor, that these two boys who had excellent character as far as I can find out before entering the service of their country, are very young and the depravity to which they have sunk undoubtedly has been brought on by reason of their youth and the environment while engaged in the service of their country.

"Might you not use your clemency, your Honor, and give to these young men at least an opportunity to think over the crime that they have committed by giving them life in the penitentiary at hard labor rather than death in the electric chair. This would be such a consolation to their respective families who are decent Christian people and who are shocked because of what has happened. I would appreciate your giving this matter your serious consideration and, meanwhile, I shall pray hard that God will inspire you to give these unfortunate youths this chance to live and pray and meditate for the rest of their lives."[3]

Getting no response from the governor, Father Flanagan traveled to Mississippi the day after Christmas 1944. While there, he spoke at a state religious conference where he was challenged for his desire to see the two boys' sentences commuted to life in prison. "One great big fellow, whom I challenged in his statement, got up and was going to do me bodily injury," Flanagan later wrote to his friend, the Rev. John O'Brien. "Of course, I very coolly told him that such philosophy and such an attitude was not in keeping with the Gospel of Jesus Christ and that as long as people manifested such an attitude we would have strife and contentions and murder."[4]

In a letter to a Meridian, Mississippi, man, Father Flanagan laid out his reasons for interceding on the boys' behalf. He pointed out that the two youths had stellar records before entering the service and that something must have happened to change their behavior. "The training which they received and which was destined to make of them strong, iron men – a training to fit them for combat service with a dangerous enemy – this training did something to these two boys. I know that in ninety-nine percent of the cases in this training the result is as desired, but apparently in a small percent of cases it reacts to the detriment of the one receiving the training.

"I would assume you would say these boys were sick boys, mentally and spiritually. That is a safe assumption to make. They were suffering some defect – something lacking in their training that other fine boys absorb – and lacking this something, this certain vitamin, these boys would be classed among the sick mentally and spiritually."[5]

On December 27, Father Flanagan dined with the governor and spoke with him in private for several hours. At the end of their conference, Bailey told the press: "I am not in the position to make a statement until the morning. I have promised to confer with one more person before I announce my decision."[6]

Interviewed at his hotel after meeting with the governor, Father Flanagan said: "I came down here on my own initiative and at my own expense to bespeak a word on behalf of two youths who committed a terrible tragedy that is unexplainable. I don't think any psychiatrist in the world could give a reason for this tragedy because the boys themselves are ignorant of why they did it...I certainly would not want to be the one to convict and say they should die in the electric chair. I realize the responsibility of the governor, and realize the many requests made on him to see that justice be done. But justice is a word often times abused."[7]

The next day, the governor made it clear he would not commute the boys' sentences. The execution would proceed. That night, Joseph Leemon wrote a brief note to Father Flanagan:

"Before you receive this no doubt but what I will be executed, but I want to thank you for your efforts towards saving my life. I deeply appreciate what you did. Father Flanagan, I am happy to say I have made my peace with my God. I have no fear of death."[8]

The December 29 edition of the *Jackson Daily News* described the execution. "Not once during their last hours did the two youths lose their composure. During their trip from the Meridian jail where they were held to Waynesboro, they spent the time singing snatches of popular songs and laughing."[9]

According to the paper, Leemon was the first to be escorted to the electric chair. He said, "I am ready to die. I am not afraid and I hope to meet everyone in heaven. Tell Mom to hold up and be brave."

Shimnick was next and, according to the newspaper account, he asked a local evangelist, "How did Joe go?" He then told witnesses, "I feel God is on my side and that's why I'm grinning." The first shock failed to kill Shimnick. He was given a second shot of electricity, four minutes later, that finally killed him.

Father Flanagan returned home to a storm of protests against his efforts to get the boys' death sentences commuted. Most letter writers told him the executions were none of his business and he should not interfere. He responded to one letter by stating, "Christ did not come to earth to punish the wicked. He came to teach. He came to show his love for suffering and sinful humanity. He came to lift up the human race from its lethargy of sin and its suppressed state of slavery under Satan. Who are we that we should cast the first stone against a fallen man or a fallen woman?"[10]

A New York couple chastised him for trying to be a "giant" and taking on causes that weren't his own. "I do not want to be a giant in anything," he replied. "All I want to do is to try and carry out in my life the teachings that I have received at my mother's knee and to put into practice those principles which my faith calls for."[11]

Father Flanagan added that he assumed the writers believed in simple justice; two boys had killed a man and should be executed for it. He asked if they had thought about the possibility that the boys' military training had somehow gone terribly wrong and influenced them to commit the murder. "These boys missed the principle and they utilized the training they received to kill a peaceful citizen. Who are you or I that should say that these boys are not mentally and spiritually sick? Who are we that should dare to say that they should be killed for their crime, instead of cured and rehabilitated back into society? I fear you are shouting with the crowd, 'Crucify Him, Crucify Him!'"

Father Flanagan wrote to the parents of both boys expressing his condolences and his frustration that he could not save their lives. To the parents of Murice Shimnick, he wrote:

"The strange thing I found in my meeting with people down there, and particularly the intelligent people, was that everyone wanted these boys to be electrocuted. I didn't find one, outside of the Catholic Priests, who felt that life imprisonment should be given to them. I fear for that kind of revenge. It is destructive. It is dangerous. It is the kind of thing that destroys security for the future – for peace. It is the kind of thing that begets miscarriage of justice, which makes for brutality and bestiality, revenge, punishment. In other words, Christ is not permitted to enter the picture, and these are people who are constantly talking about religion and Bible study and Bible class and Church. But, my friends, there is no religion in their hearts.

"I returned a broken man in spirit because of my failure, but I am happy that I tried. I would do it all over were it necessary."[12]

For Father Flanagan, the choices were simple. Follow your principles. Do the right thing. Don't worry about taking an unpopular stance. It was a philosophy he had followed for decades and would follow for years to come. He would continue to fight social injustice, religious intolerance and racial prejudice.

This philosophy helped form his attitudes about rehabilitation and second chances. It was crystallized in his oft-repeated belief that, "There are no bad boys. There is only bad environment, bad training, bad example, bad thinking."

CHAPTER

1

The Boy from Ballymoe

LEABEG HOUSE LAY IN THE SHELTER of a hill, just below the crest as it sloped gently down to the river two hundred yards below. The grasses grew tall around the house, which rested in the shadow of several large trees. Shielded from the harshest of the Irish wind and rain, it was home to John and Nora Flanagan and their eleven children.

Typical of many of the homes at that time, it was built of white-washed limestone and covered with a thatched roof woven from river reeds. There were two large, open fireplaces; one was used for cooking and the other featured a kettle where hot tea was always ready for an unexpected visitor. The fragrant smell of burning peat, the common fuel used for both cooking and heating, filled the house. The house was just thirteen feet wide and forty feet in length with wooden floors and flagstones around the fireplaces. Inside were bedrooms and a small sitting room, but the kitchen was the center of activity. It was where family members and guests told stories and sang songs.

The Flanagans were a musical family, according to Father Flanagan biographer, Gilson Willets. "There was a fine melodeon, a piano, a violin, a flute and a concertina. Each Flanagan child was encouraged to play at least one instrument. The usual practice time was one hour before breakfast. Some evenings there would be singing of folk songs and hymns."[1]

It was into this idyllic setting that Edward J. Flanagan was born, on July 13, 1886. It was a tumultuous year in the histories of the two countries that Father Flanagan would call home. In America, the famous Apache warrior Geronimo surrendered for the last time, the Haymarket Riots erupted in Chicago and the French presented the Statue of Liberty to the United States. In Ireland, the Land League was in full swing and the bill for Irish Home Rule was presented to Parliament for the first time, by English Prime Minister William Gladstone. This was the closest the Irish had come to independence in several centuries and the mood of the country was one of excitement and anticipation.

Only a few decades had passed since the horror of the Potato Famine when, from 1845–1849, one and a half million people died from starvation or disease and another million left Ireland forever. The famine affected nearly every corner of Ireland including the small village of Ballymoe, just three miles away from Leabeg House. In the half parish of Ballymoe, the national census showed a twenty-two percent decline in population between the years 1841 and 1851.[2]

In 1847, Quakers visited the workhouse in Castlerea, a larger town near Ballymoe. They reported there was a shortage of bedding and clothes, and ailments such as measles and fever ran rampant. Joseph Crosfield, in the Quaker publication "Distress In Ireland," wrote, "In the children's room was collected a miserable crowd of wretched objects, the charm of infancy having entirely disappeared, and in its place were to be seen wan and haggard faces, prematurely old from the effects of hunger and cold, rags, dirt and deformity."[3]

John and Nora Flanagan survived the Potato Famine; John as a teenager and Nora as a toddler. The Irish did not talk about the famine, but they never forgot those years that helped to shape behavior for generations.

Carmel McCaffery, in her book, *In Search of Ireland's Heroes*, wrote, "The most lamentable legacy of the Famine was the fact that it made emigration an Irish institution. It was as if an artery opened on the island and the young flowed out…The Irish born in Ireland following the Famine viewed Ireland as a land without resources, a country without a present or a future. One out of every two people born in Ireland, between 1830 and 1930, left the island to make a permanent home elsewhere. It would take more than one hundred years for the country to begin to recover socially and economically."[4]

Although his motives were different, Edward J. Flanagan would one day join these masses that left Ireland.

It wasn't just the legacy of the Potato Famine that affected Irish culture and society in the 1880s, the struggles for land rights and Home Rule were coming to the forefront. The Irish Land League was founded in 1879 and its purpose was to help to organize tenant farmers, reduce prohibitive rents and eventually assist tenants to become landowners.

The Land League also fought the eviction of tenants by absentee landlords. Considered even worse than the landlords were the opportunistic farmers who took over the farms of evicted tenants. Charles Stuart Parnell, a member of Parliament from County Wicklow who was the driving force behind this nonviolent movement, proposed that offenders should be punished by ostracism. "When a man takes a farm from which another had been evicted, you must shun him on the roadside when you meet him, you must shun him in the streets of the town, you must shun him in the shops, you must shun him in the fairgreen and in the marketplace, and even in the place of worship, by leaving him alone, by putting him into a moral Coventry, by isolating him from the rest of his country as if he were a leper of old, you must show your detestation of the crime he has committed."[5]

One of the first victims of this aggressive tactic was in County Mayo, the county just to the west of the Flanagan family's County Roscommon. His name was Capt. Charles Boycott and he was the English agent for a Mayo landlord. Boycott evicted some tenants for nonpayment of rent that resulted in his entire family's ostracism from the community. It also added a new word, boycott, to the English language.

The other prominent Irish issue in the late 1800s was Home Rule. Parnell, the Parliament member, championed Home Rule. According to *The Oxford Companion to Irish History*, Home Rule envisioned an arrangement whereby England, Scotland, Ireland and Wales, "...would have a common sovereign, executive and national council at Westminster for the purposes of statehood in the international arena, while each country would have its own parliament for domestic affairs."[6] Essentially, what the Irish were seeking was autonomy and a measure of independence.

This was the political climate into which Edward was born. It was passionate, it was volatile and, in the end, it was the failure of these dual causes that would foster more conflict and emigration.

John Flanagan was a devout Catholic and active in the work of his church. He was in his mid-fifties when Edward was born. "He was of commanding appearance, extremely conscientious and keenly aware of the responsibilities attendant on raising a family. He wore a beard throughout his life and at the time his son Edward, was born, the beard was a flaming shade of auburn which turned to the dignity of white in his advanced years. He was a stern, but just, disciplinarian."[7]

Nora Flanagan was more than a decade younger than her husband. In Ireland, men tended to wait until they were more financially established before they married. It was a marriage arranged by the two families. Willets described her as "…an exceedingly kind, generous woman and, like her husband, a devout Catholic whose valiant faith and unceasing attentions to her children earned their lifelong admiration."[8]

Her attention and caring saw Edward through the first major crisis of his life when he was just a few weeks old. He went into convulsions and his tiny body turned blue. It was only his mother's care, and the family's prayers, that saved him. It was also the first incident in Edward's lifelong struggle for good health.

According to local historian John Brady, the child population in Ballymoe during the late 1800s was three times larger than modern times. This was despite a high infant and child mortality rate. "It is possible to read in records of the time of a child absent from school having died that morning from scarlet fever, diphtheria or measles. Even some strains of flu were a hazard and there was always the threat of tuberculosis, which ravaged many families, and especially the young."[9]

Grandfather Patrick Flanagan also may have been involved with the care of the infant. Although he died when Edward was young, Grandfather Flanagan, through stories passed down by the family, would influence his grandson throughout his life. Grandfather Flanagan was a huge and powerful man admired and respected throughout County Roscommon. Although he had no formal education, the local people considered him a gifted healer and he treated both people and animals with his homemade remedies. His simple faith and belief in the healing power of prayer, was a lifelong source of inspiration for Edward.

The boy also drew inspiration from his siblings, especially from his older brother, Patrick, who preceded him into the priesthood. He was the eighth child in a family of eleven. He had five older sisters, Mary Jane, Nellie, Kate, Susan and Delia, as well as two older brothers, Patrick and James. He also had two younger sisters, Nora and Theresa, and one younger brother, Michael. Only Mary Jane and Kate were destined to stay in Ireland. Everyone else in the family would eventually leave Leabeg House and the village of Ballymoe.

The countryside surrounding Ballymoe, near the borders of counties Roscommon and Galway, would have consisted of approximately thirty town lands of varying sizes, according to Brady. "A town was the smallest division on which civil and church affairs were organized and averaged a few hundred acres each. Land tended to be organized by town land. Some big estates were divided into smallholdings and rented out to tenants; some were managed largely as stock farms."[10]

John Flanagan was a "herd," or overseer, for a mid-size stock farm of about three hundred acres. The estate's owner was an absentee landlord who rarely visited. He relied on John Flanagan to make sure everything ran properly. His judgment and expertise were essential to the success and profitability of the farm. He had responsibility for the health of the stock and fencing, and probably had some responsibility for buying and selling. Due to this prominent position, the Flanagans would have been considered prosperous by the standards of the day. John Flanagan's opinion on land rights has not been recorded, but it certainly would have been an important issue for him.

He would have considered himself not just an employee, but a steward of the land.

He also was proud of his home. "The Flanagan home was in reality a masterpiece of old world landscape gardening."[11] There were rustic walks and flower beds and stone walls of unique design crossed by numerous stairs built into these walls. These stairs allowed easy passage from one field to the next. The gardens contained flowers such as fuchsias, daffodils, rhododendrons, roses and violets.

The fields outside the garden held their own treasure. In addition to shamrocks and Hawthorne hedges, mushrooms flourished. "Each morning before breakfast it was an established routine in the Flanagan home for three or four of the children to go forth into the nearby fields and gather mushrooms, still damp from the morning dew."[12]

Following breakfast, family members would complete their assigned chores and children of school age would trek off to school. Edward began formal schooling at age five. He attended the Drimatemple National School nearly two miles away from Leabeg House and midway between his home and Ballymoe. The two-room school held forty students. Catholic teachers taught a state-approved secular curriculum and a religious program approved by the Catholic Church. They also prepared their students to receive the sacraments.

The curriculum was rigorous, with an emphasis on the classics. Irish was not taught, but most of the population was bilingual, speaking Irish at home and English at school. Edward's older sister Kate taught at this school and had some of her younger siblings as her students.

When just eight years old, Edward expressed his desire to become a priest. Willets wrote that a traveling priest, during a visit to Leabeg House, predicted the future of each of the Flanagan children. For young Edward, he predicted the priesthood and a long and useful life.[13] To prepare himself for religious life, Edward added an intensive course in Latin to his other school studies. It was taught by his parish priest, who would remain a good friend and mentor for many years.

Attending Sunday Mass was usually the only time the Flanagan children visited Ballymoe. The exceptions would have been on special occasions, including the arrival of visitors or on holidays such as Christmas. According to Brady, the church Father Flanagan attended was built in the shape of a cross. The pews were simple and unadorned. There were some special seats near the altar that were designated for certain families and their rights to those seats were always respected. Ninety-nine percent of the county's population was Roman Catholic and ninety-five percent of those physically able to attended Mass every Sunday.[14]

Catholic tradition permeated every facet of family and community life. The Catholic Church in Ireland, while conservative and traditional, was also one of the few institutions to have successfully resisted English domination. A religious vocation was considered honorable and there were more priests in Ireland than needed to staff its parishes. Because of this overflow, many priests volunteered for service in foreign missions.

That tradition of service also was strong in the Irish family. Every child in the family had assigned duties and Edward was no exception. He had suffered from a variety of ailments from a young age, so his parents decided he should avoid heavy farm work and was best suited to the less strenuous work of shepherding. When he was twelve, he took the flocks out alone for the first time.

A shepherd had to be vigilant at all times. Ireland did not have many natural predators, but there were other dangers awaiting the sheep. The system of dividing pastures was to dig a ditch and pile the earth up to one side. On this pile of dirt, which acted as both windbreak and fence, landowners planted hedges. Generally, they were Hawthorne hedges, but blackberry briers also would grow on the dirt piles. A shepherd's task was to keep the sheep in the open pasture. If they wandered to the hedges, sheep could become entangled and, unless quickly rescued, would hang there, suffering from hunger and thirst, until they died.[15]

Father Flanagan, in an April 1942 letter to his friend, the Rev. Michael O'Flanagan of Dublin, recounted those early years: "You also may not know that I was the little shepherd boy who took care of the cattle and the sheep. That seemed to be my job as I was the delicate member of the family and good for nothing else, and with probably a poorer brain than most of the other members of the family. I was sent away to school to study for the Priesthood, as I stated above, I wasn't much good for anything else; so my job as a shepherd boy fitted in very nicely in preparation for my life's work afterward. Three times a day would I travel over those immense lands of Leabeg. You have no idea what it was like with dangerous bogs on the north and south as I would travel through those vast fields, mostly without shoes – and I was a happy Irish lad, saying my rosary as I went along, and other times, as I grew older, reading one of Dickens's novels."[16]

This work – in the fields and in the classroom – put immense strain on Edward's fragile health. At the age of thirteen, he sometimes arose during the night and wandered the house reciting his Latin lessons, even though still fast asleep.

Edward's life wasn't filled solely with work and study. Just down the hill from Leabeg house was the River Suck. It was there that Johnnie King, who worked for the Flanagans, introduced Edward to fishing. It was a sport he would enjoy all his life. King and Edward would catch perch and trout using worms or flies for bait. Edward could not have had a better tutor as King was considered the fishing champion of southern Roscommon.[17]

After dinner, in addition to the music, there were stories of Irish mythology, the Firbolgs and Tuatha de Danaan, Queen Maeve and Cuchulain. Johnnie King told many of the stories. He could play music and dance the jig, and he loved to tell stories about the "little people" and the mischief they caused.[18] Just before bedtime, the whole family would gather and recite the Rosary, bead by bead, followed by prayers of thanks and for safety.

Growing up on a farm offered Edward "...a great range of useful opportunities. Chores were plentiful, varied and ongoing. He would have learned, for instance, to conduct the regular check and care of stock; both sick and healthy, to rear an annual supply of fuel in the bog, or to tend to a tillage plot where much of the family food was produced. All of these demanded patience and persistence and, as well as effort, a sense of consequence, a consideration for the needs of others and an ability to cope with adversity. His father's occupation ensured that he lived in a milieu that oozed care and responsibility. Farm activity would ensure that his disposition was tempered with tenacity and above all, perseverance."[19]

In autumn 1901, Edward entered Summerhill College in the Atlantic Seaport town of Sligo, located about fifty miles north and slightly west of Ballymoe. He was fifteen years old.

Summerhill College was the Diocesan College for the Diocese of Elphin and would be the equivalent of a private high school in America. This suggests that Edward's grades were exceptional and that his family could afford the tuition.

The College of the Immaculate Conception was founded in Summerhill, Athlone, in 1857 and was transferred to Sligo in 1880. In 1892, the college's main building was formally opened. Built of gray limestone, the imposing multi-story structure sits perched atop a hill. Today it is surrounded by a residential area, but in Edward's time it was isolated. Despite its official name, the college always has been popularly known as Summerhill. For many decades it catered to both boarders and local boys, and essentially operated as a junior seminary for the Diocese of Elphin.

Compared to Leabeg House and Ballymoe, Sligo was bustling. Its narrow cobblestoned streets may have unsettled Edward, who was more used to dusty country lanes. The noise and activity, the urban poverty and the natural beauty of the countryside all combined to create a sensory overload for him.

Summerhill College was Edward's first introduction to institutional life. It could be a lonely place for a boy away from home for the first time. Discipline was strict and punishment, in keeping with the times, could be harsh. Students could be expelled for minor infractions, such as smoking.

A schoolmate of Edward's, William Gilbert, wrote, "In those days the weather ran on more orthodox lines than at present and it was the usual thing to have three weeks of frost and snow when we returned in January after a sixteen-day holiday. The heating system in the College was utterly inadequate. The pipes were not installed until 1903, and all we had was a number of antiquated stoves."[20]

When Edward was a freshman, one of the school's upper-classmen was a young man named John F. McCormack. Although he went on to international renown as the first of many famous Irish tenors, McCormack got his start at Summerhill. "After Dinner," Gilbert wrote, "we marched round the square with John F. leading the way, and playing popular tunes on a mouth organ.

"At Benediction, we often sang without accompaniment; John F. being the leader. When we came to the Laudate, he usually struck a high key and finished alone. Though we never imagined that he had a voice that was destined to charm the world, we loved to hear him sing at college concerts."[21]

Edward, while never matching McCormack's musical success, had a fine baritone voice, and sang in the choir at Summerhill and at other schools he attended. His services were in demand wherever there was a choir and he was available. Edward was on the track team his freshman year until he suffered a bad ankle sprain. After that, his athletic endeavors were limited to handball.

"What few hours of spare time he had were spent on the handball courts, or reading, or walking around Sligo. In search of solitude he would sometimes go down to Rosses Point, where the deep-sea fishing smacks tied up and captains smoked their long pipes and reviled the English."[22]

His focus was study, and in that he excelled. Edward graduated at age eighteen, earning honors in Greek, history and geography. At a ceremony praising the college's honor students, the local bishop, the Most Rev. Dr. John Joseph Clancy, told the boys: "It is of paramount importance that, at this stage of your career, when the mind is the most impressionable, and the heart most easily swayed by external influences, your conduct should be so regulated that you will be found in conformity with right, reason and religion. If at this time of your lives you train yourselves in the important art of self-control, subduing your internal imaginations so as to subordinate them to the principles of faith and morality, then there is laid in your minds and hearts the most solid foundation of future progress and success both here and hereafter."[23]

CHAPTER

2

Preparing to Do God's Work

EDWARD FLANAGAN WAS EIGHTEEN in 1904 and armed with a degree. He was more than six feet tall, slender and raw-boned with light hair and intense blue eyes. His family expected that he would follow in the footsteps of older brother Patrick and enter the seminary.

In January 1904, Patrick Flanagan graduated from the Dublin Seminary and was ordained a priest. He was sent to do missionary work, helping to build a parish in America, in far away Omaha, Nebraska. Edward's older sister Nellie also was living in America, in New York City. She returned to Leabeg House for a visit in the spring of 1904 and spoke excitedly about New York City and life in America. She also proposed a small change in the family's plans for Edward.

Rather than sending him on to the seminary in Dublin, why not let him return to America with Nellie and finish his studies there? After all, Patrick already was a priest in America and that country certainly held more opportunities for a young man than Ireland ever could. John and Nora Flanagan thought long and hard about sending their son to America. In the end, they decided, for his future, he should go.

Like so many young Irish men and women before him, Flanagan prepared to leave everything he knew and loved behind him. Perhaps, family and friends held an "American wake," a custom where they came to say goodbye to a person they never expected to see again. All that is known for certain is he boarded the *S.S. Celtic,* of the famous White Star Line, and headed for New York City with his sister and brother.

It was the high tide of European immigration to America and hundreds of immigrants entered New York Harbor each day. It was a voyage that wasn't luxurious or without risk. Flanagan arrived in New York on August 27, 1904, just two months after more than one thousand people, mostly German immigrants, were killed when the steamship *General Slocum* caught fire and burned in the East River.

Most of the new immigrants lived in tenements on the lower east side. Conditions were terrible. Families crammed into small spaces and, in the spring of 1904, landlords had just raised the rent by twenty to thirty percent. "What is to become of the family whose sole breadwinner earns 60 cents a day and whose rent has been increased from $8.50 to $13 a month," asked one resident.[1] Flanagan was more fortunate. He wasn't taken to the tenements on the lower east side. His mother's family, the Larkins, lived in the Yonkers area of New York City.

Flanagan stayed with his relatives in Yonkers for a few weeks. The big news locally was anticipation about the opening of the New York City Subway, scheduled for October. While he enjoyed his time in New York, Flanagan was eager to continue his studies. He wrote to the rector of St. Joseph's Seminary in Dunwoodie, New York, and asked to be admitted, but he was told he needed more college credits. On October

1, he enrolled at Mount St. Mary's College in Emmitsburg, Maryland.

Mount St. Mary's College had been founded in 1808 by the Rev. John DuBois, a refugee from the French Revolution. Dubois had arrived in America in 1791, bearing a letter of introduction from the Marquis de Lafayette who had served with Gen. George Washington during the American Revolution.

By 1904, when Flanagan arrived, Mount St. Mary's College offered a program where boys and young men could study in preparation for entry into a major seminary. That first semester, tuition and fees for Flanagan totaled $170.

After his first year at Mount St. Mary's, Flanagan was evaluated by his professors as, "…a nice, decent Irish boy. Kindly and friendly – talent only fair, but he works well." They wrote that he came from a nice family and was, "…a nice little gentleman, but delicate in health and nervous about his condition. He is just fair in talent and visits too much."[2]

In June 1906, Flanagan graduated from Mount St. Mary's College with a Bachelor of Arts degree. He was reputed to be one of its youngest graduates ever, earning a degree a month before he turned twenty. Upon his graduation, Flanagan was adopted by the Archdiocese of New York as a potential seminarian. He immediately applied for entry to St. Joseph's Seminary in Dunwoodie.

In a letter to St. Joseph's, Thomas M. Mulry, president of the Emigrant Industrial Savings Bank in New York City, wrote: "This will introduce my cousin, Edward Flanagan, who wishes to apply for admission to Dunwoodie. He has just received his diploma from Mount St. Mary's. I spoke to his Grace about Mr. Flanagan two years ago and he advised his taking the courses which he has just completed. Anything you may do for him will be gratefully appreciated."[3]

The Rev. Thomas Myham, a priest at St. Ann's, the Flanagans' home parish in New York, also wrote to St. Joseph's, saying that Edward Flanagan desired to enter the seminary and belonged to an "...excellent family and will make a worthy priest. I take pleasure in commending him to your kind consideration."[4] Flanagan also received a letter of support from the Rev. Msgr. Denis J. Flynn, president of Mount St. Mary's College. He wrote that Flanagan had "shown most positive indications of a vocation," and he "wished him every success."[5] The letters of support must have worked. Flanagan was admitted to St. Joseph's Seminary in September of 1906.

The mission of St. Joseph's Seminary was to "form and educate men to serve as priests of Jesus Christ for the Archdiocese of New York, other diocese, and religious communities."[6] It was founded on May 17, 1891, by Archbishop Michael J. Corrigan, who wanted to have the state's seminary closer to his home in New York City. It took five years to finish building the seminary, constructed in the Dunwoodie section of Yonkers. The seminary enrolled its first students in the fall of 1896. The first ten years, St. Joseph's was under the direction of the priests of the Society of Saint Sulpice. In 1906, the year Flanagan began his studies, it reverted to the control of the Archdiocese of New York.

St. Joseph's Seminary dominates the top of Dunwoodie's Valentine Hill with extensive grounds covering forty acres. Its buildings are constructed of gray granite, most of which was quarried on the Seminary's own land. In Flanagan's second year at St. Joseph's, 1907, a residence wing was added to the main building.

In the spring of 1906, a few months before Flanagan entered St. Joseph's, his brother James, and sisters Delia and Theresa left Ireland and emigrated to America. His mother and father stayed behind to settle their estates, sell their home and pass on family possessions, including the great round mahogany dinner table to daughter Kate. That September, Nora and John Flanagan, along with their children, Nora, Michael and Susan, sailed across the Atlantic and rejoined the rest of the family in America.

Flanagan, never in the best of health, struggled with a variety of illnesses during his first semester at St. Joseph's. While there, Flanagan met Francis Patrick Duffy, who would become a household name as the chaplain of the "Fighting 69th." Formed during the Civil War and comprised almost entirely of Irish immigrants, the 69th New York had a sterling record during the Civil War. Its soldiers also fought in the Spanish American war and Duffy was their chaplain during that conflict. However, Duffy became famous for his work as chaplain of the Fighting 69th during its service in World War I. The story was immortalized in a 1940 movie, *The Fighting 69th*, starring James Cagney and featuring Pat O'Brien as the indomitable Father Francis Patrick Duffy.

Of course all this fame was many years in the future and Flanagan knew Duffy as his professor, mentor and friend. It was a friendship that would endure until Duffy's death in 1932.

Monsignor Aloysious Dineen, who would follow Duffy as chaplain for the Fighting 69th, was a classmate of Flanagan's at St. Joseph's. According to Flanagan biographers, Will and Fulton Oursler, Dineen remembered his classmate "...as a raw boy, although those years in Emmitsburg had begun to polish down the edges. He was not a longmouthed fellow, but a very thoughtful one. His eyes could look right through you and never even see you when he was busy in his dreams. And I can tell you this – no one in Dunwoodie during the brief time he was there would ever have voted Flanagan the one most likely to succeed. I think the majority view would have been that he would wind up as a pastor of some little country parish, where the world would never hear of him."[7]

Much of the time while Flanagan was at St. Joseph's, his health was poor. His lungs were never strong and his doctor warned that unless he rested, he could contract tuberculosis. He suggested that Flanagan head west to a healthier climate.

Matters worsened during the 1906 holiday season when Flanagan was afflicted with double pneumonia and bedridden. Throughout the second semester, he continued to take classes and complete his schoolwork, much of the time while confined to his bed. Duffy was at Flanagan's bedside many of those nights helping him with his studies. At the end of the spring semester, Flanagan took his doctor's advice and headed west to Omaha to be with his family and to recover his health.

His brother Patrick was in Omaha as the founding pastor of Holy Angels Parish. So Flanagan's mother and father traveled with him from New York to Omaha to help care for their frail son. The change in climate seemed to make a difference and Flanagan's health began to improve. While in Omaha, he received a letter from the New York Archdiocese releasing him to the Omaha Diocese and the supervision of Bishop Richard Scannell. Bishop Scannell, believing that Flanagan's health was much improved, decided to send him to Gregorian University in Rome to continue his studies. He arrived in Rome on October 4, 1907.

At Gregorian University, Flanagan took classes in dogmatic theology, moral theology, church history and Hebrew. He concentrated on his studies and ignored repeated warnings not to push himself too hard. It was a severe winter in Rome and Flanagan's rooms were cold and damp. After only a few months in Rome, Edward was forced to leave and return to the United States due to ill health. He returned to Omaha in February 1908 determined to recover and continue his studies.

This time, Flanagan did not rush his return to school. He took a job as a bookkeeper for Cudahy Packing Company, created by Michael Cudahy and his brothers in 1887. The company flourished and was one of the nation's largest packing houses by the time Flanagan became an employee. He worked there for almost two years, recovering his strength and gaining business experience. He saved his wages and planned for the day when he could return to his studies.

In autumn 1909, armed with determination and his doctor's permission, Flanagan traveled to Austria to attend the University of Innsbruck. The university was founded in 1562 and is the third largest in Austria. In 1857, a dormitory was established for seminarians from around the world and from the 1860s forward, seminarians from the United States attended the university. The dormitory, called the "Nikolai-haus," was Flanagan's home. The dormitory became so crowded that, in 1911, a large new building, the "Canisianum" was constructed to house the seminarians.[8]

The crisp, cold mountain air was a tonic to Flanagan and he enjoyed his three years at Innsbruck. The water at Innsbruck, according to Willets, turned Flanagan's hair from blond to dark brown. It also caused it to begin thinning.[9]

Back in Omaha, brother Patrick kept close tabs on his younger brother. "Each year the student's health would weaken under the strain of studies and then, when vacation time came, he would build it up again...at the expense of his brother in Omaha who paid the bills while Edward made tours of Central Europe and Switzerland, drank and bathed at famous spas and rested in the shadow of the Alps. These vacations were a highlight of young Edward's early life."[10] For years afterward, Flanagan would tell vivid stories about this time in his life; stories about mountain climbing and a visit to the world-famous passion play in Oberammergau, Germany.

According to the records of the University of Innsbruck, Father Flanagan was ordained as a subdeacon on July 12, 1912; a deacon on July 25, 1912; and a priest on July 26, 1912. All three ordinations were held at the Jesuit church in Innsbruck. Flanagan was selected, out of a class of more than 100, to say his first Mass on July 27, 1912, at the Canisianum for his fellow seminarians.

After spending most of his meager savings on gifts for his family, Father Flanagan started a circuitous journey home. His first stop was Munich, followed by a trip to Berlin before continuing on to Hamburg where he caught a boat for America. He was met in New York by his sisters Nellie and Susan, who had traveled from Omaha. He spent several days with relatives in New York before the three siblings headed west to Omaha to visit the parents Father Flanagan hadn't seen in three years. On August 26, 1912, he said his first Solemn High Mass at Holy Angels Church, where his brother Patrick was pastor. Just two weeks later, he was sent by Bishop Scannell to his first parish, St. Patrick's in O'Neill, Nebraska.

Many of the small towns in Nebraska were founded and settled by immigrants from Western Europe. There were towns such as Wilber, founded by the Czechs; Oakland, founded by Swedes; and O'Neill, founded and settled by the Irish. It was named for Gen. John O'Neill, who immigrated to the United States in 1848 and fought in the Civil War for the North. He was a fervent Irish nationalist and twice led an army of Irish-Americans into Canada in a futile attempt to trade a conquered Canada for a free Ireland. Following his disastrous invasions of Canada, O'Neill embarked on a plan to bring Irish immigrants from New York and Boston to the plains of Nebraska. He founded O'Neill in 1874. The community became the county seat of Holt County and an important cattle shipping point for the railroad.

Father Flanagan must have felt at home in this town full of his countrymen and serving at a parish named after Ireland's patron saint, St. Patrick. A picture remains of Father Flanagan from those days in O'Neill. He is tall and thin, wearing a heavy coat and a fur cap to protect him from the Nebraska cold. He stands among a group of his parishioners and is flanked on one side by a horse and buggy and, on the other, by an early automobile.

The pastor at St. Patrick's was Monsignor Michael Cassidy. Cassidy was overly strict and required absolute obedience from his subordinates.[11] Father Flanagan was paid twenty-five dollars each month and was expected to pay expenses from his salary. If he broke a dish, he had to pay for it. The Ourslers wrote that Cassidy was "a white-haired priest, devout and silent, who spent a large part of each day in prayer and meditation. At mealtimes, Father Flanagan often recalled, their conversations consisted mainly of a greeting and a few words about the state of the weather."[12]

As an assistant pastor, Father Flanagan was responsible for many duties in his far-flung parish. "Parish calls, sick calls, administering the Last Sacrament, straightening out family quarrels, kept the new curate on the go eighteen hours every day. Several mission chapels had been established in outlying regions, and it was the job of the assistant pastor to visit these missions to celebrate Mass. He would make his rounds in an open buggy, sometimes traveling thirty miles a day. In winter months the snows piled up two or three feet deep, but these trips still had to be made. Sometimes his legs and arms would be nearly frozen."[13]

His time in O'Neill ended quickly. The first signs of spring were starting to appear when Father Flanagan was transferred back to Omaha on March 15, 1913. He was appointed assistant pastor at Omaha's St. Patrick Church. Just ten days later, tragedy struck.

It was Father Flanagan's first Easter as a priest and he must have been excited about celebrating Mass on the holiest day in the Catholic church year. Easter Sunday began under cloudy skies, but had brightened around noon. In the afternoon, the skies darkened again as a massive storm moved into Nebraska from the west. According to the March 24, 1913, edition of the *Omaha World-Herald*, "death and destruction unparalleled in the history of Omaha traveled with a terrific tornado which mowed a wide and gruesome path through the city late yesterday afternoon. A balmy spring day typical in its fleeting glimpses of the sun and threatening of showers, developed into a driving rainstorm and then, in the twinkling of an eye, into a devastating monster of annihilation. And as the dead were carried to the morgues and the maimed moaned from the wreckage, and the yellow sky glowed with the carmine reflection of hundreds of burning homes, it was recalled that it was Easter Sunday!"[14]

When the storm had passed, more than one hundred

people were dead, almost four hundred people were injured and nearly seventeen hundred homes were destroyed. Gov. John Morehead called out the militia and, while touring the scene of destruction, said, "This is enough like my conception of hell to suit me!"[15]

The worst of the damage was confined to the central and northern part of town, but the storm affected the entire city. Father Flanagan had returned to Omaha just in time to witness this natural disaster and to help the town rebuild. He worked with St. Patrick's pastor, the Rev. John T. Smith, to help parishioners who had been affected by the tornado.

He also began to work with the homeless who frequented downtown Omaha. In 1913, "the city was a place of shifting population. As hundreds poured in each month, seeking jobs with the railroads, in the stockyards or the meat-packing plants, there was always a pool of the unemployed, many with families, in hungry need."[16]

That summer, heat and drought had punished the Midwest. Kansas was hit hard by the weather and crops began to fail. Many of the farm workers were itinerant and drifted with the crops, harvesting each one in turn before resting during the winter. With the crop failures hitting Kansas, these men turned north looking for work. They found conditions devastating throughout the region. They began to drift into Omaha, their traditional wintering spot, in large numbers and several months early.

Father Flanagan saw them standing on street corners. He saw they were haggard and destitute. He helped to find them food when he could, but he knew it wasn't enough. With winter coming on, they needed a place to live. He began working on an idea – a hotel for homeless men.

CHAPTER
3

Inspired by a Boy
Who Needed a Home

IT WAS EARLY DECEMBER 1915, and World War I raged in Europe. The *Omaha World-Herald's* front page featured a story of an American collaborator on trial for supplying arms to German ships. Buried inside the newspaper on page eleven was a brief story about plans for the opening of a "Workingman's Hotel."

The St. Vincent De Paul Society had leased the old Burlington Hotel and planned to operate a home for "down and out" men. The society, according to the story, would run the hotel and then turn its management over to a local priest. The hotel would sleep sixty men and feed one hundred. "Just how the home will be managed has not yet been decided. One idea is that businessmen will buy tickets and then hand them to applicants entitling them to a bed and meals. But the plan of management, it is thought will be agreed upon long before winter sets in."[1]

The priest selected to manage the Workingman's Hotel was Father Edward J. Flanagan, assistant pastor at St. Patrick's Church in Omaha. He was twenty-nine years old.

Father Flanagan didn't realize then, but the frustration he would feel trying to help these men would inspire him to found a home for wayward boys that would help to change the way America took care of its troubled youth.

In mid-January 1916, the hotel opened. Located at Eleventh and Mason Streets, it had been furnished and remodeled through donations. The residents were to pay ten cents for a bed and five cents for a meal. The unemployed could stay for free, but only with Father Flanagan's permission.

In 1915, it was estimated there were between one thousand and fifteen hundred homeless men in Omaha. Demand almost immediately outstripped the hotel's capacity of forty beds. Within a month, Father Flanagan asked for sixty more cots, along with clothing and shoes. Father Flanagan did not want his hotel to be merely a "flop house" for homeless men. He wanted to change lives, to get men started on new careers. He worked with local businessmen to help find work for his residents. In that first month, according to *The True Voice*, Omaha's Catholic newspaper, he found jobs for twenty men.[2]

Some of his first boarders were itinerant farm workers looking for refuge in the winter months when there were no farm jobs. These men were used to working for a living, but they had been reduced to living in old boxes and coal bunkers along the railroad. Father Flanagan's Workingman's Hotel was a godsend. It was open twenty-four hours a day and a rough camaraderie soon developed among the men.

The men elected "shoppers" who would appeal to the local packinghouses for stew meat and the bakeries for day-old bread. Local grocers often provided vegetables. The only food the shelter needed to purchase outright were staples such as coffee, sugar and milk. Some of the men with cooking experience prepared the meals for the others. That first winter passed and, in the spring, many of the farm workers returned to the road and their itinerant lifestyles. Their places were taken by a different sort of man. "Whereas the first groups of men were either jobless or homeless, the second group consisted mainly of a class of men whose problems in life defied solution," Father Flanagan recalled. "Their characters were depraved, they were indolent and few of them cared what the morrow might bring."[3]

In September 1916, Archbishop Scannell transferred Father Flanagan from assistant pastor at St. Patrick's Church to assistant at St. Philomena. Within a few weeks, he began working full-time at the hotel. The new residence was now providing three hundred men a home. In the next fifteen months, Father Flanagan and his supporters would find 1,551 jobs, many temporary, for the men. Father Flanagan's log showed 25,259 lodging nights provided, nearly half of which were free.[4]

When the farm workers returned in late fall of 1916, they found the Workingman's Hotel had changed. It had become a two-tiered facility. The basement of the hotel was now reserved for the rougher class of men. The others called it "The Lower Regions" or simply "Hell." When a drunk would stumble in, the men would march him straight to "Hell" to be washed, sobered up and made comfortable for the night.

One night a denizen from "The Lower Regions," objected to Father Flanagan's attempts to take a bottle of liquor from him. He picked up the young priest, carried him outside the door and threw him over a ten-foot fence. Because Father Flanagan was six-feet tall and 180 pounds, this was no mean feat. Suffering only a slight cut over one eye, the priest returned to find a crowd of his regular residents making it clear to his assailant he was no longer welcome.[5]

A rough set of rules and regulations began to develop, and some of the men took it upon themselves to help run the day-to-day operation. This left Father Flanagan free to mingle with his guests and talk to them about their lives and what had brought them to the hotel. These men's life stories fell into predictable patterns. Most were at least thirty years old and some were decades older. Almost to a man they had spent years wandering across the country. They were living rough, they were out of work and they were cynical. They simply survived; their main goal was to find a hot meal and a warm bed.

He discovered something else – almost all of them had a similar upbringing. Father Flanagan explained his thoughts: "I knew…that my life's work lay in the rehabilitation of those men. And yet, my methods were so basically wrong… In talking with the men, I learned that they had been orphaned in childhood… Or were members of large families where income was not sufficient to care for them… Or again, they might come from families broken by divorce. Invariably, they were homeless and abandoned… They veered here, were shoved there throughout their formative years and, reaching a man's estate, they were only shells of men… I knew that my work lay not with these shells of men, but with the embryo men – the homeless waifs who had nowhere to turn, no one to guide them." [6]

Father Flanagan realized that few of the men who stopped at the hotel thought of it as anything other than a temporary refuge. He had given his heart and soul to this work, but most of these men would not remain with him long enough for him to make a difference in their lives. They had developed deeply rooted habits that seemed impossible to change.

He wondered if his residents would even remember his Workingman's Hotel a year later. It was convenient, but no different from places they had been in cities throughout the country. He looked at the small percentage of men he had been able to place in jobs and compared it to the majority who came for a few days or weeks and then simply moved on. He was frustrated by his inability to make a difference in these men's lives.

Occasionally, a young boy would wander into the Workingman's Hotel. He might be ten or twelve, but he tried to act older and tougher. He tried to give the impression that he didn't really need help from anyone. But, of course, that was exactly why he had come to Father Flanagan's hotel.

Father Flanagan talked to these boys and listened to their

stories. Some he reunited with their families, some he helped to rescue from the juvenile court system. Many boys had spent time at reform school that did more to provide an education in the criminal arts than to offer any true rehabilitation. Father Flanagan knew that a boy without friends or family to support him was helpless in the courtroom. He began to seek cases in juvenile court and would do what he could to help these boys. He analyzed their stories and compared them to the residents of his hotel. He saw hope for these children. Not yet fully formed, they could be molded and shown a new way of life, a different way of living.

He did not see these boys as criminals. They were poor, ragged, abandoned. They were hungry. They were just boys and they needed shelter. Many had served time and that stigma was attached to their names. Father Flanagan believed that these boys needed a home – someplace they could grow, learn a trade and live in safety. It was too late for most of the men in his care, but it was not too late for these boys.

Father Flanagan began to speak to his friends about creating a home for boys. He told them about his hope for these children and his belief that he could make a difference in these young lives. Excited by his dream, he told of his plans to create a place that was not a reform school or a youth prison. It would be a new concept, designed not simply to warehouse children, but to give them a second chance.

When the farm workers returned to Omaha in the fall of 1917, they found Father Flanagan hard at work designing and planning for his new home for boys. Instead of using his time trying to reform men already set in their ways, Father Flanagan decided to work with destitute and abandoned boys. He would try and mold them into productive, honest citizens.

Years later, Father Flanagan related a story about a young boy who came to his Workingman's Hotel. "One evening, about the time I was closing my hotel for the night, the door opened and a boy stepped in and closed the door. His clothes were ragged and torn and his cheeks were red with the cold.... In his little voice he asked: 'Are you the man who runs this place?' On being answered in the affirmative he said: 'Would you please let me stay here for the night. I won't bother you and I promise I'll go on tomorrow. I'm awfully cold and if you'll just give me a corner I'll be satisfied.'"[7]

Father Flanagan arranged for the boy to stay in a small room used by the watchman. He would be safe and segregated from the homeless men. He gave the boy some sandwiches and a glass of milk.

After ensuring that the boy was safe for the night, Father Flanagan retired to his room. He wrote, "I turned on the one light which gave off a faint glow. The room was bare. Even the broken window had been patched with a piece of cardboard. The wind moaned and some place in the building a loose board hit back and forth. I thought I must get that fixed tomorrow. Silently I took my prayer book and knelt in prayer. As I knelt down, I thought about these men and me and the boy, I thought of my home. My kind mother and father. My brothers and sisters. How good and kind they all were to me. I thought of the time I was 14 and remembered the teaching of my good mother. Her love and kindness for those about her. How she would always, by teaching and example, impress on my mind the great happiness in life – love for those about you, especially those who are less fortunate than you. How I yearned to have her close to me. She could help this boy. And then the picture of her faded from my mind and I saw the tear-stained face of the boy. The one who had asked for a corner. Innocence and youth – unspoiled. I must help this boy and others like him. God had sent me one of his little ones to show me the way... I vowed then and there that from that day on with God's help I would try, in my humble way, to guide the footsteps of the boys who had no father and mother. I would try and give them the teachings my father and mother had given me. And all of this when God sent me one of his own to open my eyes."[8]

Father Flanagan knew his home would be nonsectarian – open to homeless boys regardless of their race or religion. It was the same principle he had used in operating the Workingman's Hotel. Today, this nonsectarian policy seems standard, but in 1917 it was revolutionary. The United States was a society segregated on lines of gender, income, faith and, especially, race.

He researched orphanages and other homes for children, examining their strengths and weaknesses. Every institution he examined put limitations on the class of children it would help. Homes that were operated by fraternal lodges, for example, were only open to boys who fit narrow criteria. Orphanages usually were maintained only for younger children or for infants. There were no homes for adolescent boys that he could use as a model.

Father Flanagan's dream was to create a home for older boys where they could be given the care, education and training they so desperately needed. He wanted to create a community where boys could learn to work and to play. Somewhere they felt safe. A place they could call home.

Father Flanagan was not content to wait for boys to come to him. He would seek them out. The juvenile courthouse seemed a good place to start. The only "crime" many of these boys had committed was being homeless. The judges often had no choice but to send them to reform schools. Father Flanagan did not blame these judges. They knew the reform schools were often merely training schools for young criminals, but their hands were tied.

Many of these boys had already suffered abuse at the hands of brutal parents or guardians. Some had been abandoned by their parents or orphaned by the untimely death of a mother or father. A local judge told Father Flanagan, "These boys don't need punishment – most of them need three square meals, a clean bed and someone interested enough to give them care and an education. What am I to do with them? They come into court after some little trouble and what am I to do and where am I to send them? I can't send them home. In many cases, that would be like sending them back for more trouble. Many of them have no homes. What can I do, Father?"[9]

Father Flanagan thought he had the answer. Now all he needed was a chance to prove it. It came one morning in the late autumn 1917 when several frightened boys were brought before a judge. Their ages ranged from twelve to fifteen. After listening to the charges brought against them, Father Flanagan asked the judge if the boys could be paroled in his care.

The judge gave his reluctant consent and Father Flanagan walked out of the courtroom surrounded by the boys. They looked to him expectantly, waiting for his direction. He walked with them to a nearby vacant lot and began to talk about what they would do. He was careful to avoid talking about the past. He talked only of the future. They agreed to meet every evening. But Father Flanagan wanted more for his boys. He petitioned Archbishop Jeremiah James Harty, who had recently succeeded Archbishop Scannell as the head of the Omaha Archdiocese, to relieve him of his duties at the Workingman's Hotel so that he could concentrate on helping these boys and the many others who would follow.

Finding a Home

ON A CRISP, AUTUMN DAY in 1917, Father Edward J. Flanagan was riding in a street car with his friend, Leo Hoffmann, and a young real estate agent named Catherine Shields. He mentioned that he was looking for a big house in which he could establish a home for young boys. Shields knew that the Byron Reed mansion, on Twenty-fifth and Dodge Streets, was available for rent at ninety dollars a month. Father Flanagan asked to visit the property and was delighted with the possibilities it presented.[1]

In 1917, ninety dollars was a large sum of money. Still, few people spent it more wisely than Father Flanagan. That ninety dollars paid the first month's rent on the house and started a home that in the coming years would give thousands of troubled youth hope for a new and better life.

Many different stories evolved over time about the identity of the donor who gave that first ninety dollars. However, it is all but certain that Henry Monsky, a prominent Jewish lawyer, was the person. He asked Father Flanagan to keep his gift anonymous, and Father Flanagan never publicly revealed the donor's identity. However, his sister, Nellie Flanagan, stated that the donor was a Jewish friend of her brother.[2]

Monsky and Father Flanagan had been acquainted for several years and both men shared an interest in the welfare of children. They may have first met in the Douglas County Courthouse at the trial of some young boy, both intent to do what they could to help. However they came together, a friendship developed between the Catholic priest and the Jewish lawyer. Neither man felt constricted by the borders of religion. They simply wanted to help children regardless of their race or religion.

When Father Flanagan talked about his dream to help

troubled boys, his friend Monsky was one of the first to volunteer to help. Monsky went on to become the international president of B'nai B'rith and the chairman of the American Jewish Conference, but he never forgot his friend, Father Flanagan. He served as a member of the Home's Board of Directors for many years.

According to newspaper accounts, the weather on December 12, 1917, was "unsettled with probable snow and continued cold."[3] The big, warm house must have looked inviting when Father Flanagan and two boys walked up to the door. After dropping off the first two boys, Father Flanagan returned to the courthouse to pick up three more. Waiting to greet those boys were Father Flanagan's staff, two nuns and a novice from the School Sisters of Notre Dame. They were assigned by Archbishop Harty to assist at the home.[4]

The home was furnished in a slap-dash style with odds and ends of donated, mismatched furniture. The chairs around the dining room table varied widely in age and design. "The meager supply of chinaware, the knives and forks and spoons formed a rag bag, a junk box of kitchen equipment. So, too, on the second floor; a chaotic jumble of beds, cots, blankets and spreads brought into orderly usefulness in the dormitories."[5]

One of those first boys, in a letter written to Father Flanagan during World War II, recalled that first day. "That morning in December of 1917 is indelibly stamped into my brain. I can never forget how, after the juvenile authorities had relinquished my brother and I and we were in your custody, you presented me with a bag of chocolates and I felt pretty good about it even then.

"When we got to your home on Twenty-fifth and Dodge and you had introduced us to Sister Rose, who then showed us our room, I remember how you had to rush away without even so much as a bite to eat."[6]

When he wasn't working with his boys, Father Flanagan was writing solicitation letters or raising money in other ways. He struggled to have enough just to keep the door open and the boys fed. Local judges continued to send more and more boys to him. After the first week, fifteen boys resided with Father Flanagan, and another ten had moved in one week later, by Christmas Eve.[7]

Christmas Eve in 1917 was an uncertain time at Father Flanagan's home. There would be no feast of turkey, ham, and mashed potatoes and gravy for the boys. In fact, there wasn't much food at all. That evening, a local merchant delivered a Christmas surprise to Father Flanagan – a barrel of sauerkraut. Each boy could have a second helping.[8]

Father Flanagan knew that if he was to be successful, he had to establish his boys' home in the hearts and minds of the citizens of Omaha. He needed to educate them on what he was trying to accomplish and he had to show them how they could help these troubled boys. He created a newspaper. Not only could he raise money by selling copies of the paper, but he could use it to inform the public about his home and to lay out his revolutionary philosophy of youth care.

The first issue of *Father Flanagan's Boys' Home Journal* appeared in February 1918. It featured poems, tongue twisters and jokes. The lead story explained Father Flanagan's philosophy for caring for boys. In an article titled "Boys' Home," Father Flanagan wrote, "What to do with the delinquent boy is a question that has troubled the minds of those interested in the future citizenship of our progressive city. His parents, for one reason or another, have lost control of him. He no longer respects their authority, or, at least, his actions do not seem to be guided by their wishes and commands… Notwithstanding all the boys' mischievous and wayward acts, still, perhaps he is not what we would ordinarily term a bad or vicious boy."[9]

Father Flanagan added he was in favor of reform school for those who were a "menace to a community of peace-loving and good-living citizens." However, he didn't think it was a fit place for boys who were "full of the pranks of a boy" and without enough common sense to keep themselves out of trouble.

"For this class the Boys' Home, just started a couple of months ago, has been a God-send. It furnishes all the comforts of a Home. It takes care of the temporal and moral needs of the boys. It gets away from the idea of a Reform School, and the boys who reside there feel the relief of being able to breathe the refreshing air of confidence on the part of those in charge.

"This Boys' Home is open for all boys, regardless of Creed or Nationality, and it only suffices that the boy is in need of some guiding influence, and a friend who will take a personal interest in his guidance."[10]

Father Flanagan continued to lay out his philosophy in subsequent issues of the *Boys' Home Journal*. In the March 1918 issue he wrote about the "Boy Whom Nobody Wants." He described misunderstood boys whom some found difficult to control. "His appearance is not, as a rule, attractive, and he may show signs of the wear and tear of great negligence… But somehow, we feel this boy ought to have a chance. He is young, and no one can tell but, in that little neglected lad, there may be qualities which, if properly drawn out, might develop into a great man who may one day brighten up the world by his service to God and humanity."[11]

Father Flanagan wasn't attempting this transformation of troubled boys by himself. In addition to his dedicated staff, a group of women, the Ladies Organization of the Boys' Home, volunteered to help. They raised money for the home and helped with cleaning, cooking, washing and sewing. "These ladies deserve the highest praise for the beautiful spirit they manifest in taking up this most necessary work, and the enthusiasm which they instill into others."[12]

In addition to Father Flanagan and the many volunteers, the boys were expected to contribute. They had assigned chores around the home and many helped by selling the *Father Flanagan's Boys' Home Journal* on street corners and after Mass at local parishes.

For most of the boys, this was familiar work. Many had scratched out a living working as "newsies" for the *Omaha Bee* and the *Omaha World-Herald.* The two newspapers conducted fierce circulation wars, complete with quotas and stipulated that their "newsies" sell only their paper or risk losing their street corner.[13]

According to a 1920s study by the U.S. Department of Labor, newsboys lived a bohemian lifestyle. "Without supervision except that of the street circulators and truck drivers, the boys smoked, played cards and craps and carried on other forms of gambling. Cursing and vulgar language were common, lying and stealing were regarded as jokes and news of an arrest was a signal for the crowd to repair to the police station."[14]

Local newsboys faced competition from "hobo newsies." These were young men who had run away from home or were out to "see the country by 'bumming rides.'" According to the Department of Labor report, "Most of them would not work and sold their papers only long enough to get a free bed and earn a few dollars for food; others, though professional hustlers, were too restless to stay long in one place and spent their time 'bumming' their way from city to city wherever they heard that a paper was booming its circulation."[15]

These older boys were accused of "dishonest and unwholesome" practices by the younger newsboys. "They urged the boys to practice various tricks on the public in order to sell papers, and themselves set the example and boasted of it. They taught the boys to gamble and kept them playing cards all night cheating them and taking away their money."[16] There were even reports of some of the younger newsboys being "used by the hobo newsies for immoral acts."[17]

Father Flanagan knew these young boys needed to be removed from this dangerous environment. He helped as many as he could. In marked contrast to their former lifestyle, he found a practical, healthy use for their street skills.

"All of our boys, with but a few exceptions, had been 'on the job' before, selling papers, and some of their faces, no doubt, were familiar to our readers. Then, they were known as 'newsies,' with their characteristic street manners, with voices shrill and loud, with language unfit for any decent person, with faces unwashed, perhaps for days; with clothes which now they would be ashamed to wear. Today they appeared not on street corners, but at various churches, beaming with smiles and proud in their Sunday attire; proud that today they could hold their own as little gentlemen, clean, polite, graceful."[18]

Now that he had been operating his home for several months, Father Flanagan began to understand the differences between taking care of men and taking care of boys. With men, he worried mostly about supplying them with food and shelter. With boys, Father Flanagan believed he had a responsibility to help educate them. Initially, he sent them to area schools, but they weren't always willing to admit his boys. He realized he would need his own school, and he knew he needed more room.

As word spread about Father Flanagan's home, more and more boys began arriving at Twenty-fifth and Dodge Streets. Some were sent by kindly judges and other just heard about the home on the street. The home was soon full and Father Flanagan needed a larger house. A fundraising event was to be held on April 11, 1918, to raise money for new quarters.

The fundraiser was to be an "informal dance" with a forty-piece orchestra and band music. "It is the hope of those in charge of the entertainment to raise about ten-thousand dollars and that the same will be a start for a New Home Fund. Our present quarters are entirely inadequate and demands on the home are so great that we cannot do justice to the work unless we can secure larger and better equipped quarters."[19] Father Flanagan didn't have to wait long for a larger home to present itself.

Nearly a year before, April 6, 1917, the United States had declared war on Germany and entered the conflict known as World War I. Germans were the largest immigrant group in Nebraska and even had their own German language newspapers in Omaha. With America's entry into the war, anti-German fervor swept the country, and Omaha was no exception. One result was the closing and abandonment of the German-American Home, a large mansion at 4206 S. Thirteenth Street.

Father Flanagan arranged to rent the German-American Home, and his boys soon filled it with energy and laughter. Through public support, he was able to open a school in the home and hire qualified teachers to help him run it.

Many of Father Flanagan's boys were behind in their schooling because they had missed classes due to sickness, poverty, truancy and imprisonment. "The boys disliked going to school in Omaha because in the city schools they were frequently belittled by the other children because of their clothing or because they were backward in their grades."[20]

By providing his own school, Father Flanagan was able to assess each boy's educational needs and design an individual program to suit those needs. It not only helped the boys to progress, but also empowered them.

In addition to teaching the boys to read and write, Father Flanagan wanted to make his home self-sufficient. Having come from a farm background, he believed the boys could be taught some valuable life lessons by doing farm work. Friends donated a cow in hopes of supplying milk for the home. Unfortunately, these were city boys and no one knew how to milk it.

"An elderly neighbor, upon learning of Father's predicament, came over and taught some of the older boys how to milk a cow. Whenever the boys milked the cow, many of the others would stand around and admire the process and then proudly carry the pail of milk to the kitchen every night and every morning."[21]

Some chickens also were donated to the home, but they refused to stay put and the boys were "constantly chasing around the neighborhood to retrieve the runaways."[22] His boys were interested in farming, but Father Flanagan realized that operating a farm in the heart of the city was a difficult task. He began to think that the only solution was to buy land on the outskirts of Omaha and move his home for boys to the country.

Living space was another factor driving the need to relocate again. Within a few months after moving to the German-American Home, Father Flanagan was caring for one hundred boys. As more boys arrived, sent by the courts or simply coming on their own, the population of the home would soon swell to its limit of 150 boys. Father Flanagan feared he would be faced with the unpleasant task of telling boys he had no more room.

Feeding and providing clothes for his current residents were difficult enough. With the country in the midst of a war effort, money was tight. In the *Father Flanagan's Boys' Home Journal,* Father Flanagan wrote, "In addition to the demands which the war makes on us, we have other great responsibilities, which we must not overlook or neglect, otherwise our social life might become greatly impaired. Our institutions of charity which are caring for the sick, aged and infirm, for the young and the old, must be supported."[23]

Father Flanagan's summer fundraising appeal had not been successful. The home had only a two months' supply of coal to last through the coming winter months and the boys needed warm clothes and new shoes. In a story titled, "Our Needs," he appealed to his donors. "We have cared for some three hundred boys since the Home was opened last December, and the influence and moral training which these boys have received have put a ray of hope into their neglected little souls, and many of them today are out doing their part and are making good… I know, kind reader, if you were to know our needs and the scanty means we have to care for them, you would assist us. We shall leave the matter to your judgment to decide what you will do to help us in caring for these 'lads whom nobody wants.'"[24]

September of 1918 brought new trouble to Omaha. An epidemic, believed to have begun in the Army barracks in Fort Riley, Kansas, began to spread across the nation. It was called the Spanish Flu because it was thought to have originated in Spain and then been transported to the United States by soldiers returning from Europe. Nationally, at least one American in four fell victim to the disease. In Omaha, one of the first places for the flu to appear, public gatherings were banned.[25] Most frequently, children ages five to fourteen were flu victims.[26]

According to a newspaper account, about fifteen thousand cases were reported in Nebraska.[27] When the epidemic ended, nearly 500,000 Americans, and many millions of people throughout the world, had died.[28] The Spanish Flu orphaned many American children, adding to the increasing numbers of homeless children.

In the December edition of *Father Flanagan's Boys' Home Journal*, Father Flanagan wrote about the dual tragedy of the war and the Spanish Flu. "Today the hearts of the Christian world are sapped with grief and sorrow over the awful bloodshed and carnage of millions, and the terrifying plague which is now claiming so tremendous a tribute of lives. There are very few homes in Omaha that have been so fortunate as to escape either of the two great causes of grief and many of them have had reason to suffer both."[29] Father Flanagan's home was no exception. One of his boys succumbed to the epidemic and died.

The flu epidemic added to Father Flanagan's decision to look for a cleaner, healthier environment for his boys. The combination of a lack of space and a desire to remove the boys from the influences of urban life prompted him to decide on an eventual move to the country. "He wished to take his boys to a real farm where they would have ample room to play. He wanted to find a place where they would have a home, which they felt was theirs and not just a rented building.

"One evening at the supper hour, Father called his charges around him and asked their opinion regarding a home in the country. Their response was a chorus of shouts of approval, and they immediately began asking when and where it would be."[30]

Father Flanagan made finding a farm for the boys a high priority. "One of the great problems which confronts our work for boys is the need of a permanent Home which we could call our own and from the experience in the work up to the present time, we feel that we can best help the boy by giving him plenty of work to do outside of his regular school work. Our present quarters have already proven to be ill fitted for keeping the boys as busy as we would like, and although seemingly spacious, are not suited for furnishing the most needed employment. We need a farm of medium size, which would solve the labor problem, and while at the same time furnishing good, healthy exercise away from city life, with its temptations, also assist toward supporting the home… We are convinced beyond doubt that the securing of a farm home for this class of boys would work one of the greatest blessings for the caring of the delinquent and homeless boys of our city."[31]

In June 1919, Father Flanagan's success in helping delinquent boys prompted the Omaha City Council to appoint him to its Public Welfare Board. Two months later, August 5, 1919, he achieved a quiet milestone of his own, becoming a citizen of the United States of America. He was now officially an American and determined to do everything he could to help the children of his adopted country.

The first farm Father Flanagan acquired was in the Florence area, on the northern edge of Omaha. He bought it for fourteen thousand dollars in September 1919, according to the warranty deed. The land, which formerly was a chicken farm, included twenty acres and was called Seven Oaks Farm. He immediately began to raise money to build up the property.

"Our newly acquired farm has given us new hopes and

greater ambitions; the farm, however, is not ours yet. We borrowed almost all the money to pay for it and our indebtedness amounts to $12,000. If we had this debt off our mind, we could begin figuring on our building… Our new home should have a capacity of one hundred and fifty boys, and were it not owing to our present limited quarters, we would have that number in our home now."[32]

Father Flanagan quickly realized that the farm at Seven Oaks was too small to fit his needs. In February 1920, he sold it to the Sisters of Notre Dame for the price he originally paid. The land later was developed into Notre Dame Academy, a private school for girls.

Father Flanagan used the fourteen thousand dollars he received from the Notre Dame Sisters to pay for another plot of land, called Forty Acres. It was located about two miles west of Seven Oaks property, near Forest Lawn Cemetery. He kept chickens and cows on the farm, which supplied eggs and milk for his boys. The boys considered it a great privilege to take the streetcar from the German-American Home north to Forty Acres and pick fruit for Father Flanagan's Boys' Home.[33]

As more boys arrived at Father Flanagan's door, not everyone was happy. Some boys had been in trouble with the law, many were homeless and no boy was turned away because of his religion or his race. Some Omahans were not pleased with this tolerant attitude. "A few referred to it as Father Flanagan's 'Reform School' for young thieves." Others criticized the policy of white, Chinese and Negro boys living together without segregation.

"'If God had intended people to be all the same,' one Omaha politician demanded, 'why did he make them of different colors?'"

Father Flanagan's reply: "'And could you tell me – what is

the color of the soul?'"[34]

During this time, Father Flanagan realized he needed help running his home. The Sisters did what they could, as did the Mothers' Guild. His nephew, Patrick Norton – son of his oldest sister, Mary Jane, and recently graduated from Creighton University – was eager to help his uncle. In the summer of 1920, Norton was appointed superintendent of the farm and as a general assistant to Father Flanagan at the German-American Home. Norton would work at Boys Town for more than four decades until he retired in 1978.

Father Flanagan believed he would need around $300,000 to build a permanent home for his boys. A generous gift of ten thousand dollars from Mrs. E.W. Nash gave the building fund its start and the *Father Flanagan's Boys' Home Journal* provided monthly updates about the campaign.

In July 1920, the home received its first prominent visitors: Archbishop Daniel Patrick Mannix and Bishop Daniel Foley from Australia and Eamon De Valera, the president of the newly created Irish Republic. During the visit, De Valera and Father Flanagan began a friendship that would last for decades.

Father Flanagan kept busy coming up with ways to spread word about his Home and to raise money. He created a traveling troupe of young entertainers and the Knights of Columbus sponsored a statewide tour of Nebraska. "The troupe consists of five of our boys accompanied by Father Flanagan himself, and the program will be made up of many interesting and entertaining features showing the great blessings that our Home has brought to so many poor and unfortunate boys. Accompanied by the entertainment will also be a moving picture of the life of the Home, which will, also, be most interesting."[35] This traveling troupe would lead to a traveling music show and, eventually, the famous Boys Town Choir.

Throughout this time, Father Flanagan continued to accept more boys. One story has endured – the story of a young boy dropped off by his mother in September 1920. His father had abandoned him and his mother was no longer able to care for him. As the boy sat in the shadows, his mother pleaded with Father Flanagan to take care of her son and promised to send money for his care whenever she could. Father Flanagan agreed to take him and his mother kissed her son and quickly walked out the door.

When Father Flanagan rose and beckoned the boy to follow him, the boy was unable to rise from his chair. He could not walk. Although the Boys' Home was not equipped to help disabled children, Father Flanagan could not abandon the child. "It's all right," said Father Flanagan. "You'll have a great time here. One of the bigger boys will carry you up to your room where you'll stay with the other fellows."[36]

The young boy's name was Howard Loomis and he soon became popular around the home. The boys competed to see who would have the privilege of carrying him. In a photo in the August 1921 edition of the *Boys' Home Journal*, Loomis is shown being carried "piggyback" by another boy. "Reuben Granger is the lucky 'horse' in the picture, but it was only by clever strategy that he obtained the role, for there is a continual 'battle' among our older boys for the privilege of carrying little Howard."[37]

More than a decade later, Father Flanagan's memory of Granger carrying Loomis on his back would help to inspire Boys Town's famous slogan, "He ain't heavy, Father, he's m' brother."

In 1921, Father Flanagan faced two challenges: overcrowding at the German-American Home and its owners' decision to have Father Flanagan vacate the building. "The owners of our present rented quarters have informed us that we must vacate just as soon as it is possible, owing to the fact that the building is needed by them for other purposes…We are now facing a serious situation, and the only solution of the problem is that we must build, and begin to do so immediately."[38]

The chicken farm at Seven Oaks had been sold to the Sisters of Notre Dame and the farm at Forty Acres was proving to be too hilly and without enough tillable acres to be a productive farm. On May 25, 1921, Father Flanagan agreed to pay $100,000 for 160 acres of land ten miles west of Omaha. He swapped Forty Acres, along with some cash, for the down payment. The remainder would be paid in installments. It was 160 acres of mostly tillable land and already had some farm buildings on it. Called Overlook Farm, it seemed like the solution to Father Flanagan's problems and the answer to his dreams.

"One of the finest farms in Nebraska, it has 89 varieties of fruit trees, five varieties of grapes and is stocked with cattle, horses, calves, pigs, chickens, etc…. The 13 buildings are all of the most modern structure, and the barns, piggeries etc., are all provided with concrete floors, running water and electric lights.

"Beautifully located on a hill, the farm will provide a splendid setting for the new home and will afford our boys plenty of room to play and the finest of fresh air and sunshine, so necessary to their growing bodies."[39] A committee was quickly formed and a campaign launched to raise $300,000 to erect and equip a dormitory for the boys. The foundation would be built in June, and Father Flanagan hoped to have the building completed in ten months. Finally, in October 1921, it was time to move.

"Roads have been laid, railways constructed, cities built and moved by the labor of men, but we doubt if ever more willing hands were put to labor than those of our hundred boys in moving from their old Home to Overlook Farm.

"For months they had talked and dreamed, 'Overlook – Overlook – Overlook, will we ever get there?' Every boy who was so fortunate as to visit the farm prior to moving day was plied with questions as to how it looked, what was being done, and above all, 'When do we move?' Father, on his return each day while the temporary quarters were being constructed, was surrounded by a rushing crowd of boys eager for new information.

"At last word came that the building would be completed on Saturday, the 15th of October, and that the Home would start moving on the following Monday. And sure enough, on Monday morning, bright and early, the first van load was off. But moving is a slow job, particularly when it is to a spot fourteen miles away. Constant work accomplishes wonders, however, and on Saturday the 22nd everything from the mice traps to the two-ton safe, the canaries to the ice box, the phonograph to the last handkerchief of the littlest boy, was safely moved and the last fifty boys were loaded onto a truck – the unwilling Carlo (our Shepherd dog) lifted in after them – and Father Flanagan's Boys' Home was officially moved from its old Home to Overlook Farm."[40]

It was probably cold for Father Flanagan's boys on the open bed truck as it rambled west to Overlook Farm. The dust and grit from the gravel road would have filled their eyes and stung their faces, but no one complained. They were going home.

CHAPTER

5

Building a Village for Little Men

FATHER EDWARD J. FLANAGAN finally had his farm. Now he had a place where his boys could grow up free from the influences of the city and could learn about the benefits of hard work.

After the initial excitement of the move had passed, the boys had time to explore their new home. Father Flanagan, in the *Boys' Home Journal*, described the event: "Do you, kind reader, remember any moving days when you were a child? Do you remember how every corner and nook of every building had to be discovered, explored and surveyed before you children were satisfied that nothing had escaped your rapacious eyes? Well then, picture over 100 boys doing that self-same thing."[1]

Now that they had the land, the next goal was to get suitable buildings to house the boys. Some existing ones could be used, but most needed to be built. Al Witcofski, who came to the home in 1920, was still young when Father Flanagan and his boys moved to Overlook Farm. According to Witcofski, five new buildings were constructed. "They were just like these old barracks you had in the army," Witcofski said. "The two buildings on the south were dormitories, that's where we slept.

The one on the end was the Rec hall and there was a classroom and a chapel. They had a big folding door that went down the middle so they had two classrooms and then the altar was on the end. The fourth building was the dining hall and the kitchen and in one end was where they separated the milk.[2]

Father Flanagan knew he would need a large dormitory to serve as the main building. The original buildings were wood-frame and heated with wood stoves. Once the five-hundred-bed dormitory was built, Father Flanagan planned to turn the outbuildings, now housing his boys, into workshops for carpentry, painting and other trades.[3]

He had a vision of offering not only traditional education, but also to help his boys learn a trade. His first two homes had little room for extras, but Overlook Farm would be different. According to an article in the *Omaha Bee*, a vocational training department would be added to the traditional education that the home provided. Father Flanagan launched a $300,000 fundraising drive in July 1921.[4]

Father Flanagan hoped for financial assistance from Omaha's wealthy. He voiced strong opinions about the responsibility of the rich to help those who were less fortunate. He believed that to many people, wealth was a "dangerous enemy," and he was more than willing to help them find a solution to this problem. "Without being conscious of its insidious influence, they permit it [wealth] to glorify them in the scarlet cloak of pompous worldliness, of an exaggerated and, often, domineering influence, using that power of money which a mere accident may have invested them in, to the detriment of the cause of God's chosen ones – the poor and the suffering. Such people lack the light of religion to reveal to them their great responsibilities, and fall short of their great stewardship."[5]

Father Flanagan knew he needed the help and good will of others if he was to succeed in his mission to help troubled boys. However, at times, his temper got the best of him. From the very beginning, his work had been criticized as well as praised. Neighborhood leaders had resisted his plans to build his home in the Florence area because many thought his boys were incorrigible. He was willing to listen to advice and suggestions, but only under certain conditions. He made his feelings on unsolicited advice clear in a short paragraph in the *Boys' Home Journal*. "Anonymous letters find no place in our file and receive no attention from us whatsoever. Anyone having anything to say in criticism of the policy of our Home, or our *Journal* – the organ of the Home, is at perfect liberty to do so, but please do so in a manly and honorable manner, and do not hide behind the degrading nom-de-plume of the anonymous."[6]

Father Flanagan was driven to expand his program. That is why he had moved to larger homes and why he had purchased Overlook Farm. He knew if he educated more people about his revolutionary youth care ideas, he could raise more money and help more boys. His home for boys was not just another reform school. There would be no walls and barbed wire around the farm. He told concerned Omahans: "I am not building a prison. This is a home. You do not wall in members of your family."[7]

Members of Father Flanagan's family now were helping him. In addition to his nephew, Patrick Norton, his mother, Nora, and sister Nellie also were helping Father Flanagan care for his boys.

His initial fundraising drive was a failure. According to the Ourslers, the reason for the failure was because he had hired professional fundraisers who didn't understand the unique nature of the Boys' Home and had used the wrong approach in the appeal. A second campaign was conceived and this time it would be run by local volunteers who knew the community and its citizens.[8]

An ecumenical group of prominent Omaha citizens formed the core of the new fundraising committee. It included a Protestant, J. D. Davidson, later president of the Nebraska Power Co.; two Jews, Morris Jacobs, who would help found the national advertising agency, Bozell and Jacobs, and Henry Monsky; and a Catholic, Francis P. Matthews, who would later be secretary of the Navy under President Truman and ambassador to Ireland.

The *Omaha World-Herald* endorsed the campaign. "The campaign which opens today to raise $300,000 for a home for Father Flanagan's boys is one of the biggest and worthiest movements to which Omaha has ever devoted itself.

"It is because Omaha has come to know Father Flanagan as a very remarkable man, who is doing a very wonderful work that this city has organized to raise for him a sum adequate to the needs of this noble cause to which he has given himself." The endorsement went on to effusively praise Father Flanagan and his work. It included a plea to help raise money so that Flanagan could take care of "500 boys at a time instead of less than 200."[9]

The endorsement concluded with a description of the importance of Father Flanagan's work at Overlook Farm. "It is a work of building clean manhood that is going on out there. It is a character university whose attendance is constantly shifting. No boy is kept there longer than necessary to give him the right footing for right living and to find a proper home for him. As each passes out into the world another takes his place. It means the rescues of thousands of boys, the fitting them to fill an honorable and useful and happy place in the world, who otherwise, most of them, would become flotsam and jetsam on the tides of life. It means the building of homes rather than additions to penitentiaries and asylums. It means a growing attendance at the churches of all faiths, a diminishing line before the police judge each morning."[10]

Of course it would take more than a stellar committee and the endorsement of a local newspaper to raise $300,000. Father Flanagan also enlisted the help of some of his boys, in particular Charles Kenworthy, who became known as the "boy orator." Kenworthy spoke at numerous meetings and gatherings, and shared his own personal experience at the Home in glowing and emotional terms. "Many an audience, having heard the 'boy orator,' rose and cheered and then emptied their pockets."[11]

Despite this hard work, the campaign was still far short of its goal and time was running out. It was then that Mrs. Arthur Mullen stepped up and organized the Women's Bucket Brigade for a final concerted push. The women formed teams of five or six, and armed themselves with buckets. They planned to go to every home and business in Omaha and ask for donations.

The women weren't afraid to go anywhere or ask anyone for help. "Downtown they invaded restaurants, stores, night clubs, pool-rooms, even speakeasies. Bootleggers and gamblers, bums and crooks in the backwash of Omaha's business section threw their coins and dollar bills into the buckets."[12]

The final effort put the campaign over the top. In March 1922, a year after they had moved to Overlook Farm, Father Flanagan and his boys broke ground for a new five-story brick building. It would include classrooms, a dining hall, a gymnasium, a dormitory, a chapel and a small hospital.

The money raised by the campaign was paid directly to the builders so funds were still needed to meet the home's daily expenses. Hiring a development staff was crucial to keeping the fundraising momentum going. In an age when few women worked outside the home, Father Flanagan, perhaps impressed with the stellar work of the Women's Bucket Brigade, took the unusual step of hiring two women, Zaida Dimond and Gertrude McCarthy, as his first field agents. The women traveled the eastern United States soliciting funds for Father Flanagan and his home for boys.

Father Flanagan knew he had to find other ways to raise money beyond relying on donations. One of his more unusual ideas was a show wagon troupe. The inspiration for the idea came from an early supporter of the Boys' Home, Dan Desdunes

Desdunes had moved to Omaha from New Orleans in 1904. In 1916, he created and trained an elite group of African-American musicians who became the official band of the Omaha Chamber of Commerce.[13] An early admirer of Father Flanagan, he volunteered to train the boys for a minstrel show. He selected fifteen of the most talented boys and prepared them for a special show in January 1921. It was a huge success.[14]

The boys enthusiastically wanted more so Desdunes formed a band and drilled the boys for many weeks. "We now have a band of thirty-two pieces that any school in the West would be proud to possess. On May 1st this band will start to tour the States through the summer months and thus help raise funds for their permanent home which is now being built on Overlook Farm."[15]

By May 1922, the band had a playlist of thirty-five songs, including "I'm Nobody's Baby," and "How Can I Leave Thee." Each band member received two pairs of khaki pants, two pairs of shoes, two pairs of coveralls, six pairs of stockings, and a raincoat and cap.

The boys first performed in Bennington, Nebraska, on May 7, 1922. Two days later, they performed in nearby Elkhorn. The boys traveled from town to town in three Pullman wagons, drawn by three separate teams of horses. The first wagon carried the boys, the second carried their beds, instruments and baggage, and the third served as a complete kitchen that was equipped with stoves, utensils, cups, plates and a pantry.[16] In those early years, other than private donations, the revenue generated by the show troupe was the only income the home had.

Along the way, the boys had plenty of opportunities to visit ice cream parlors, play games and go swimming. Some of the boys got so badly burned by the sun that they had difficulty playing their instruments and one lad was forbidden to do any more swimming because he "swallows too much water." The drum major of the group was a young African-American boy, named Oscar Flakes, who was a crowd favorite.[17]

Flakes had been brought to the home by his mother. He was from Marshalltown, Iowa. Desdunes and Father Flanagan wanted the talented Flakes in their show troupe, but his mother was reluctant to give her permission. Flakes, decades later, recalled that while he was enthused about the possibility of performing with the troupe, Father Flanagan had to convince the boy's mother because the priest "…wouldn't do anything if the parents had any objections. He wouldn't go over their head."[18]

Eventually, Flakes received his mother's permission and he headed out on the road. Father Flanagan often accompanied the boys in those first years with the show troupe. "He was a very beautiful man," Flakes recalled. "As a matter of fact, he was mother, father, everything to a young boy. He would wrestle with us, run with us, horse ride with us…do anything a youth would care to do …shoot marbles with us."[19]

As the troupe went from town to town, the boys weren't always met with a warm welcome. Flakes recalled a visit to a small town in southeast South Dakota. "We had come in the nighttime, late. When the morning came, we got up. Father Flanagan was with us then. Anyway, we boys gave our order of what we wanted for breakfast and one of the boys would take it to the restaurant and put the order in.

"At that time, there weren't too many hotels that had their own dining room. In this particular instance, we got ready to go. I most generally brought up the back end because I liked to window shop and trail along behind. So when I came into this restaurant, the fellow said he wanted the little colored boy to eat in the kitchen. Father asked him why. He said, 'Well, we don't serve any colored people in this town.' Father said, 'okay,' and we all went into the kitchen.

"And the man said, 'I don't mean all of you…just the little colored boy.' And Father Flanagan turned around and said, 'Well if the boy can't eat out there and we can't eat in here, than we don't eat here at all!' He turned around and he left the food…they had a table all set and everything, the food was all cooked and waiting for us…and he walked out."[20]

That night, when the troupe performed, the restaurant owner came and donated five hundred dollars. For the next two days, all of the boys ate in the dining room.

Sometimes the challenge his boys faced wasn't racism, but simply ignorance. Flakes recalled performing in Beatrice, Nebraska, a town where many of the community's youngsters had never seen a black person before. Many people were poor and couldn't afford the cost of admission so they provided room and board in exchange for an opportunity to see the show. "When we gave a performance at night, sometimes people would come up on the stage after the show," Flakes said. "This little girl came up to the stage and…look[ed] at me. She would walk around me and go back to her mother. Finally, she brought her mother over and she said, 'Mother, take him home and wash his face so he will be clean like me.'"[21]

Another obstacle Father Flanagan faced was the resurgence of the Ku Klux Klan. The organization, founded by Confederate Gen. Nathan Bedford Forrest in 1866 to fight against reconstruction in the South following the Civil War, had faded away by the mid 1870s. Following the release of the 1915 film, *Birth of a Nation*, which portrayed the Klan in romantic terms, the KKK experienced revitalization. It spread beyond its native South to the Midwest and West.

The new Klan targeted Catholics, Jews and foreigners, as well as minorities – which allowed it to expand its base beyond the South. Its credo not only pledged members to be "true to the faithful maintenance of White Supremacy," but also restricted the membership to native born American citizens who didn't owe any allegiance to foreign governments or to the Pope.[22]

Following World War I, the KKK launched a major membership drive in the Midwest. "The first Nebraska Klavern was founded in Omaha in 1921. By the end of the year, there were about twenty-four chapters in the state with an estimated membership of more than one thousand. By 1923, the Atlanta headquarters of the KKK claimed forty-five thousand members in the state. The Lincoln Star reported that the Klan was active in Lincoln, Omaha, Fremont, York, Grand Island, Hastings, North Platte and Scottsbluff."[23]

Father Flanagan and his mission were anathema to the Klan. Not only did he accept any boy regardless of religion, race or creed, but he employed African-Americans and women in positions of authority. To make matters worse, he himself was a Catholic priest and an immigrant.

The show troupe had at least two encounters with the Klan during its cross-state travels. The first occurred in Iowa when Pat Norton was traveling as the manager of the show troupe: "...a minister who had joined the Ku Klux Klan advised us that if we put on our show in that community, he would tar and feather all of us. He did not have guts enough to give his name. Apparently he was ashamed to be affiliated with the Klan, being a minister.[24]

The Ourslers recounted a stop in a community about three hundred miles west of Omaha. "As they rode into the village, there were no boys at the edge of town; no one came out to greet them. This was unusual, because in all the other towns officials had cordially greeted them.

"Pat Norton climbed out of the lead wagon to investigate. It did not take long to piece together the bad news. No booking had been made for them in this town, and no auditorium was available for them. Worse, from what he could gather, they had no bookings beyond this town. Because of Ku Kluxian prejudice, the advance agent had run into booking troubles and had departed for parts unknown without informing them."[25]

The troupe was out of funds and stranded. Father Flanagan gathered some money and helped the troupe limp back to Overlook Farm. That was the end of the traveling show wagons. They could only cover about twenty miles a day and the expense of feeding eight horses, eighteen growing boys and three staff members was considerable. "I believe it cost more money to take care of the horses than it did the boys," Norton recalled.[26] The show troupe continued to perform until the late 1920s but, beginning in 1923, members traveled by train.

In the spring of 1923, the band was featured for the first time on the new medium of radio when a station from Newton, Iowa, broadcast a performance by the boys. It would be the first in a long line of radio shows for Father Flanagan's boys.[27] Within a few years, Father Flanagan and the band had a weekly radio show called "Advice to Boys."

Father Flanagan realized fulfilling a goal of providing his boys not just an education, but a trade when, in February 1923, he opened a broom factory at Overlook Farm. The seventh-, eighth- and ninth-grade boys spent two days a week helping make brooms. Eventually, boys would learn other trades, including carpentry, tailoring, shoe-making and barbering. There were plenty of hands to help out as the population of the home now stood at 250 boys.

That August, John Flanagan, age ninety-four, died. His wife, Nora, came to live with her son at Overlook Farm. She added a maternal element to the boys' lives, many of whom did not know their own mothers. Al Witcofski remembers her as a "big, old Irish woman." Even with all those boys around, Nora Flanagan's son, Edward, was still the apple of her eye. "He (Father Flanagan) liked to box and everything," Witcofski recalled. "Of course you would be out messing around, boxing him and he had to hold his own. One day he was out there boxing away and he had his glasses on and one of the kids hit him and knocked his glasses off. Out she come, telling her son, 'Come on you big kid, get in the house. Get in the house.'"[28]

Christmas always had been a special time of year at the Boys' Home. In 1923, the Home celebrated its seventh Christmas. The *Boys' Home Journal* described the festivities as beginning Christmas Eve when Santa Claus rode into the gymnasium on a Shetland pony, explaining that he'd had to leave his reindeer and sleigh in the far North. "The pony made itself at home with us and while the candy, nuts and toys were being distributed, went among us as if to make our acquaintance." After enjoying a Christmas feast and toys sent by generous donors, the boys watched a movie.

"You could hardly believe that so much happiness could be crowded into one short day, but nevertheless we were glad to hear the bedtime signal. And after breathing a prayer for our benefactors we fell asleep to dream of friends who made possible a Christmas that will long be remembered at Overlook."[29]

By the end of 1924, 280 boys lived at Overlook Farm. As of January 31, 1925, nearly 1,800 boys had lived at the home since its founding in 1917. The boys had come from twenty-nine different states and were of twenty-five different nationalities. Sixty-two percent of the boys came from Protestant homes, thirty-five percent from Catholic homes and three percent were from Jewish families.[30]

Father Flanagan continued to add new trades for his boys. In 1924, he introduced his boys to typewriting and shorthand. In 1925, he added a printing plant. "One of the greatest improvements has been the establishment of a printing plant at the Home, where is printed all our own literature, including this magazine. Not only is it a money saving institution, but more importantly, it furnishes the basis of a splendid trade for our boys who are anxious to learn."[31]

Teaching his boys a trade was one way Father Flanagan could help to prepare them for their life after Overlook Farm. He knew this was the only real home many of them would ever

know. He also knew the fondest wish of many of the homeless boys at Overlook Farm was to be part of a family. He saw
Overlook Farm as a temporary refuge for these boys and he
found many of them adoptive parents. However, as the fame of
his Home spread, some people came with more selfish inten-
tions. They were looking only for cheap labor. After raising the
hopes of these children that they had finally found a home,
they would return them to Father Flanagan when the work
project was finished or the crop was in.

This fundamental betrayal infuriated Father Flanagan and
he wrote about it in the *Journal.* "The great desire of everyone interested in homeless children is to secure for them good
homes and the love of adopted parents. We are always happy
at Overlook Farm when we find a good home for one of our
boys, but we are also saddened when our so-called good homes
have proved to be slave-driving, soulless homes of people who,
notwithstanding splendid impressions made, and recommen-
dations brought with them, have proven a lack of interest in
the welfare of the boy, and wanted him only for what service
he could be to them. There have been too many of such selfish people, and this Home proposes to watch with the greatest
scrutiny any such adoptions from now on."[32]

As time passed, Father Flanagan began to see his home for
boys as a destination and not just a temporary refuge. The boys
had a school, they were learning trades and they grew much
of their own food. He wanted them to be independent so that
when they left Overlook they could survive in the outside
world. With that in mind, he began to explore the concept of
self-government for his boys.

The boys wanted to help Father Flanagan in this endeavor.
Three boys created a group they called the Knights of Honor.

This group would be an honorary organization that would only be open to the best-behaved boys. Each department of the Home would be under the charge of a boy manager, allowing him to gain valuable experience. Sam Madenti was elected president. "By making ourselves examples for all the other boys in the Home," Madenti wrote, "we hope to be of some service instead of being stumbling blocks in the progress of the Home. We are going to help lighten the burden by gradually assuming the whole management of the Home and thereby decrease the running expenses."[33]

At the same time that Madenti was forming the Knights of Honor, another group was pushing the idea of turning Overlook Farm into an independent village. In February 1926, the boys voted to officially change the name of Overlook Farm to Boys Town.

Now the boys had their own town and were determined to help govern it. Two political parties, the Square Six and the Wise Six, formed. There were thirty-two candidates for mayor that year, and the political atmosphere at the home was spirited with banners, speeches and bands. Anyone who was a citizen of Boys Town, could write his name and could read a ballot was given a vote.[34]

The village's structure was patterned after nearby Omaha with a mayor and several commissioners. The first election occurred on February 14, 1926. William Roach, an African-American, was elected mayor; Frank Ban, commissioner of finance; James Ban, commissioner of parks and streets; Carl Blazko, fire commissioner; Joe Laslovitch, police commissioner; and Ted Kenney, commissioner of industry.[35]

Roach was proud of his new town and wrote about it in the *Boys' Home Journal*. "The population of our town is 280 citizens, all up and going. Although our town is rather small we are not lacking in any of the facilities that are necessary to conduct a large city. We have the following industries in Boys' Town: carpenter shop, shoe shop, print shop, engineering department, laundry, canning kitchen, dairy department and last but not least, not only one, but several town bands and orchestras.

"We hold council meetings once in every week. A report of the week's activities is handed in by each commissioner. We all enjoy our work very much. I hope all our readers will join me in giving Father Flanagan a hearty vote of thanks for giving the boys this excellent opportunity."[36]

This approach was something completely new – this town populated by boys and governed by boys. This place they called Boys Town.

6

Putting Boys Town on the Map

MOTHER'S DAY COULD BE a difficult time at Boys Town. Some boys had never known their mothers, others had been abandoned or rejected by them, and many had been placed at Boys Town when their own mothers could no longer care for them. In a 1926 Mother's Day speech to his boys, Father Edward J. Flanagan spoke of the solace a mother can bring. "We are all children today. We put aside our cares and worries and in memory sit at the feet of her, who is accustomed to brush away our tears and unburden us of our sorrows, for Mother understands us better than any other person in the world, and with her, we are at peace."[1]

"No one will take Mother's place for you. No love will ever be as great as Mother's would have been. No home seems right without her gentle presence, and the world knowing this, tries to minister unto you its love and pity, and God above looks on at this merciful ministration and blesses it. Sometimes, you may find the world cold and indifferent, and lacking in its duty towards you, but if you do, it is because the world does not possess a heart that throbs for her child."[2]

Father Flanagan knew the boys' mothers were irreplaceable, but he was determined that Boys Town would be the best possible substitute. That meant providing them an education, teaching them a trade and preparing them for life once they left Boys Town. All that came with a steep price tag.

In 1926, Boys Town was burdened with a mortgage of more than $100,000, in the form of bonds that had been sold to complete the building expansion. The bonds were due in April 1927, and Father Flanagan wondered whether he would be able to pay them off. "Our struggle in the past years to carry on the work here, feed, clothe and educate our large family of homeless boys has been so great that I have been unable to set aside any money to pay off our indebtedness... Oh, it is a great worry as all of you know, but with God's help, I hope I will be able to see this debt cleared up before next April."[3] He began to include articles in the *Boys' Home Journal* about financial planning and encouraged donors to consider including Boys Town in their wills.

Father Flanagan was used to having financial challenges, but now his lack of funds meant he had to turn boys away from his Home. In November 1926, twenty-one boys were admitted to Boys Town, but more than one hundred had applied for admittance. "The Home is now taxed to its capacity," Father Flanagan wrote, "and with the winter months at hand we are going to have a hard time to keep the homeless lads, fed, clothed and educated."[4]

He initiated a "Burn the Mortgage" campaign and recruited ten chairmen to spearhead the campaign. Father Flanagan suggested that if they could get one hundred people to donate a gift of $1,000 each, his problems would be solved. He later amended that idea and said if fifty people would donate

$1,000, he could then rely on other donors to give smaller gifts to make up the difference. He justified his appeal by stating, "Is there anything more noble, more praiseworthy than helping a poor child in a constructive way to become a good American citizen?"[5]

Support for the campaign began to pour in, and letters from prominent local businessmen, civic leaders, educators and newspaper editors appeared in the *Boys' Home Journal* pledging their support. The mortgage bond holders gave Father Flanagan a ten-day grace period and, by the end of April 1927, he was able to decrease the mortgage from $103,000 to $30,000. He pledged to hold off on burning the mortgage until all debts were paid. "Although we did not raise the entire total, we believe we have had one of the most successful charity campaigns in this part of the country. We did not get one cent in pledges, for it was a cash campaign. The fact that we raised so much money in cash is evidence of the large number of friends we have in the United States."[6]

Unfortunately for Father Flanagan, the Home would continue to struggle financially until the mid-1940s when the first foundation fund was established. Throughout the 1920s and 1930s, Boys Town continued to expand. In his quest to help more children, Father Flanagan took in as many as he could and he would worry later about how he would pay for their care.

The home now had been established for several years, and his boys were succeeding after they left Father Flanagan's charge. Many found jobs in agriculture or industry and sixty-five former boys were attending colleges and high schools across the country. Boys Town was located too far from the city for the boys to attend local high schools and they had no money to pay for boarding school. So Father Flanagan instituted a program to place boys in reliable homes where they could further their education. "The more education they receive, the better their chances will be for success in this world. Any lad in our Home who wishes a higher education is given the chance. We watch over them carefully after they leave our Home."[7]

Father Flanagan had always believed in helping every child he could, and that included children with disabilities. "I remember some years ago a boy came to us from an institute for the deaf in Illinois, having been placed there by an aunt because his hearing was a little defective," said Flanagan. "The aunt evidently wanted to get rid of her charge the easiest way possible, so she put him in this institute for the deaf."[8]

The child stayed there for two years. He was compelled to learn sign language and his education suffered, because he was losing "...the gift of God – his speech," said Flanagan. "Through some friends of the boy's aunt, we were notified of the case and we took him in immediately. I had him examined by an ear specialist who pronounced his case as one of slight deafness which could have been permanently cured had it been attended to in time. With treatment, he has much improved. Last year that boy passed the eight grade county examination… is the head cornetest of my radio band and is well on his way to mastering the printing trade."[9] Father Flanagan's mission was to meet the emotional and medical needs of the children who came to live at his home. After treatment he wanted each boy to either return home or go to a foster family because he felt the best environment for a child to grow was within a loving family. Unfortunately few families came forward with the offer to foster one of the boys in their home.

While Father Flanagan's Boys' Home had hosted many famous visitors, including movie star Tom Mix and band director John Philip Sousa, none excited the boys as much as two men who visited in November 1927. Fresh from winning the World Series, Babe Ruth and Lou Gehrig made Boys Town one of their first stops on a national tour. After being introduced to the students, each player gave a brief speech and then served as captains as they split up the boys into two teams for an impromptu baseball game.

Ruth had lived in St. Mary's Orphanage in Baltimore, Maryland, so it was easy for him to identify with Father Flanagan's boys. A story in the *Boys' Home Journal* stated that Ruth "...now makes more in one year than it takes to support Father Flanagan's Boys' Home for nearly two years." Ruth told the boys to never be ashamed of having been at Boys Town and advised them to appreciate what Father Flanagan was trying to do for them. He also pledged to help Flanagan in his fight against people who treated the boys like unpaid, temporary labor, adopting them and then returning them as "unsuitable" when the season's work was done. He called it "profiteering in homeless boys," and it must have struck a deep chord in this man who had grown up in an orphanage.[10]

December of 1927 marked the tenth anniversary of Father Flanagan's Boys' Home. More than twenty-one hundred boys had passed through its doors. During those years, the Home had received no money from "city, state or church;" all of its money had come from the public.[11] It was to that same public that Father Flanagan appealed on a matter of justice and he used the new medium of radio to spread the word.

Father Flanagan was a pioneer in the use of radio for public relations and fundraising. His weekly show featured advice to families and addressed the plight of the homeless boy. One of the most popular personalities on his radio show was a young man named Johnny Rushing. Rushing became known as "Johnny the Gloom Killer" and his upbeat message soon spawned a club of admirers calling themselves the Gloom Killer Club. The famous humorist, Will Rogers, was elected as the club's first president. By the end of 1928, it had six thousand members. Their goal was to recruit twenty-five thousand members.[12]

Father Flanagan understood the persuasive power of this new medium. He saw radio as a way to get his message out without having to travel across the country with his boys. "Through the magic of radio his plea for the homeless boy would be flashed in an instant to hearth sides in a million homes up and down the Main streets of America."[13] One of his first successes was to use radio to influence public opinion in the case of two young brothers from Missouri.

Edward and Earnest Shetron were born into poverty. Their father had deserted them when they were infants, and their mother struggled to feed and clothe them. Edward was nine, and his younger brother Earnest was seven, when they decided to rob a grocery store in their home town of Thayer, Missouri. They were quickly captured and sentenced to two years in the state reformatory in Booneville. Father Flanagan was appalled at the thought of these two young boys incarcerated with much older inmates. He believed they should have been placed in Missouri's state children's home in Carrollton. However, the law specified that only children without "criminal tendencies" could be placed in Carrollton.[14]

When the two brothers arrived at Booneville they "appeared undernourished, their faces pinched from lack of proper food."[15] But they didn't act like hardened criminals. "The day they were brought here by the Oregon county officials they raced around the superintendent's office as boys on a picnic, peering into file cases and hammering on the typewriters."[16]

Father Flanagan wrote to Sam Baker, Missouri's governor, asking that the boys be removed from the Booneville prison.

"I deeply appreciate your prompt attention in looking into the case of the two Shetron boys detained in the reformatory at Booneville.

"My purpose in writing is not to find fault with the treatment accorded inmates at Booneville…but my dear Governor, these little children are only seven and nine years of age and they are in a penal institution! All the care and attention of Booneville, and for that matter the care and attention of the whole state of Missouri, can never obliterate from these children's minds the blot that society is putting in their young years by detaining them in a penal institution."[17]

He pointed out that he understood the boys had not been removed from Booneville because of "some technicality of the law." He added, "Don't you think that in the interest of humanity and for the sake of giving these mere children a better chance, some way can be found to overcome this technicality?

"These children are not criminals at heart, neither are they, I feel, inclined criminally.

"Environment will have a great deal to do with the future success or failure of these children… If your laws are so exacting, and if your Board of Pardons is so unrelenting as to not make possible the transfer of these little boys from the reformatory to the Orphans' Home, then, please, turn over these boys to Father Flanagan's Boys' Home and I will guarantee you they will grow up to become a credit to the state of Missouri; and you, my dear Governor, will have a right to be justly proud of the noble deed you did for these little ones."[18]

In addition to letters to the authorities in Missouri, Father Flanagan publicized the boys' plight through stories in newspapers across the country. He also spoke about them in his weekly radio show. The story began to capture national attention and pictures of the boys were carried in many big city newspapers. Still, the governor refused to budge, saying his hands were tied. Father Flanagan kept up the pressure through his radio show and letters of support began to flow in. In June of 1928, a year after they had been imprisoned, the "kid bandits" walked out the gates of Booneville prison, were greeted by Father Flanagan and escorted to Missouri's Home for Dependent Children in Carrollton.[19] An artist's conception of the meeting appeared in newspapers across the country, with Father Flanagan bending down to greet the two boys. His reputation as a crusader for children's rights was cemented.

For every well-publicized case like the Shetron brothers, there were countless stories about "tag boys." These were young boys who showed up at Father Flanagan's doorstep with a piece of paper pinned to their clothing saying simply, "Father Flanagan's Boys' Home, Omaha, Nebraska." They had few possessions and many didn't know or remember their parents. They had been sent along their way by well-meaning strangers who believed that Boys Town would be their refuge.[20]

There also were boys, intrigued by Father Flanagan's traveling troupe, who wanted to join up when the group left town. Willets wrote about a boy he called "Sparky" who asked to speak to Father Flanagan in one of the small towns the troupe was passing through.

"Please may I see the big man with the black hat?" Sparky asked.

He looked about eight years old, and was hungry and tired. Hearing the boy's voice outside his railroad car, Father

Flanagan responded, "Tell me, dear, what did you wish to see me about at this time of night?"

Quickly he told Father Flanagan his life story and ended with a plea, "And Father, may I go on the train with the other boys?"

Father Flanagan had heard similar requests many times and he needed to verify Sparky's story before making a decision. He asked around town and discovered that Sparky was telling the truth. His parents had both been killed in a bus accident when he was young. He had been taken in by a childless aunt who died of pneumonia just a few years after adopting Sparky. Her husband was an alcoholic who seldom worked and spent what money he did have on drink. Sparky earned a small income selling newspapers, but it wasn't enough to keep him and his uncle fed and clothed. They survived only because some kindly neighbors did what they could to help them.

After checking with the local authorities, Father Flanagan made all the necessary arrangements to take the boy with him. When the people in the town discovered Sparky was going to Boys Town, they chipped in and bought him a new set of clothes.[21]

The traveling troupe not only helped to recruit homeless boys, it also acted as a public relations tool for Father Flanagan. "My little showmen were actually pioneer missionaries in welfare work," Flanagan said. "They took the story of the homeless boy as he was, and is, and they convinced thousands of friends that a neglected and homeless boy is not a criminal. They had ample time to show the public that they were normal, happy boys, if only a home were provided for them."[22]

In August of 1928, the traveling troupe paid a visit to President Calvin Coolidge in Superior, Wisconsin. The troupe had met the president the year before in Rapid City, South Dakota, and he remembered several of the boys. A photo, taken of the boys and the president standing on the steps of a local high school, strategically included two African-American boys placed right next to Coolidge. Father Flanagan wanted to make sure his home's policy of integration was obvious. He wanted to show the world that while racial segregation was the rule in the rest of the United States, no such racism occurred at Boys Town.

By the end of 1928, 250 boys called Boys Town home, and Father Flanagan decided it was time for another building expansion. Many of the wooden barracks, built in 1921, were still in use and he was concerned about them being fire traps.[23] He wanted to replace the buildings currently being used for the trade school, for recreation and for storing equipment. The plan was for three new buildings: a gymnasium, a trade school and living quarters for certain faculty members.

By now, the Boys Town fundraising operation was well-organized. Plans were quickly made to raise the needed $250,000. "The campaign was a success from the start," Willets wrote. "Small and large contributions were received from all parts of the country. One kind friend donated all construction costs of the combined gymnasium and office building, including enough to build a fine swimming pool in the basement." In the summer of 1929, Father Flanagan broke ground for these new projects with construction expected to be completed by the spring 1930.[24] Of course, not all the fundraising was complete before construction began so a mortgage was placed on the home. It was hoped it could all be paid off soon with the help of loyal donors.[25]

The self-government policy of the Home, which began with so much enthusiasm in the spring of 1926, had proven ineffective and had been abandoned within a year. In an effort

Ruins of Leabeg House, birthplace of Edward Flanagan.
County Roscommon, Ireland.

Ballymoe, County Galway, Ireland. *1904*

Edward Flanagan, (third from the right in back row) aboard the *S.S. Celtic* coming to America. *1904*

Edward Flanagan, (at far left) mountain climbing with fellow seminarians. Innsbruck, Austria. *1909*

John and Nora Flanagan pose with eight of their eleven children including (front row, from the left) Edward, Michael, Patrick, (back row from the left) Delia, Theresa, James, Nellie, and Susan. Omaha, Nebraska. *1908*

Father Edward Flanagan. *1912*

Father Edward Flanagan (front row on the left) with parishioners at his first parish assignment at St. Patrick's, O'Neill, Nebraska. *1912*

First Workingman's Hotel. Omaha, Nebraska. *1913*

William Teninty (middle) one of the homeless boys soon to be an early resident of Father Flanagan's Boys' Home. Omaha, Nebraska. *1917*

The first home at
25th and Dodge
Streets, Omaha,
Nebraska. *1917*

Father Flanagan with residents at the German-American Home.
Omaha, Nebraska. *1919*

Father Flanagan welcomes (from the middle left) Archbishop Daniel Patrick Mannix, Melbourne, Australia; Bishop Jeremiah Harty, Omaha, Nebraska; Eamon De Valera, President of Ireland; Bishop Daniel Foley, Ballarat, Australia. Omaha, Nebraska. *1920*

Overlook Farm, the eventual permanent home of Boys Town. *1922*

With the boys' band. *1926*

Oscar Flakes, a member of the boys' band. *1922*

With Lou Gehrig, Babe Ruth and residents of the Home. *1927*

Congratulations from the boys after being selected Omaha's citizen of the year. *1933*

With residents of the Home. *1936*

Going over lines with Spencer Tracy during the filming of the movie, *Boys Town. 1938*

Spencer Tracy, Father Flanagan, and Mickey Rooney in Omaha for the premiere of the movie. *1938*

Boy Killers---Will History Repeat?

ROBERT TEMPLEMAN, fifteen, who slew his brother, and in whose behalf child psychologists and juvenile court advocates moved to save him from what they called the "bungling" in the case of the state's other boy slayer, now in the penitentiary at Walla Walla.

HERBERT NICCOLLS at fourteen, at the time he slew a peace officer, whose trial in 1931 on first degree murder charges aroused child welfare groups, who claimed he was a case for mind specialists and juvenile experts rather than for the criminal law. He was given life.

NEW DEAL FOR YOUNG SLAYER IS DEMANDED

Child Clinic Head Declares Fate Of Templeman Shall Not Parallel Nicholls Case

Mrs. O. F. Lamson, head of Seattle's child clinic, who enlisted child and welfare groups of the state in behalf of Herbert Niccolls, fourteen-year-old Eastern Washington slayer, yesterday announced that the same groups would oppose any effort to repeat the bungling of the Niccolls boy in the case of Robert Templeman, fifteen-year-old Buckley slayer.

Mrs. Lamson wrote a letter to Judge Fred Romann of the juvenile court Pierce County at Tacoma, in hose custody the Templeman now is, praising him for his statements regarding his preliminary analysis of the case and "enlightened handling of the matter to date."

'NO NICCOLLS CASE'

"We do not want to repeat the Herbert Niccolls case," Mrs. Lamson told the Post-Intelligencer. "The Templeton boy is entitled to intelligent handling, and the case should be kept in the juvenile court, not turned over to the prosecutor and the criminal courts, as was Herbert Niccolls. The boy should be carefully studied and all background and facts carefully investigated before action is taken, and we are sure Judge Romann will see that this is done.

"We did not criticize the judge in the Niccolls case. He was held to a cut and dried procedure under the criminal law when the case was turned over to the prosecutor. The mistake was made in ever letting the case get into the criminal courts. You cannot secure justice for a child in the environment of the criminal courts and the penitentiary. There is no leeway in the criminal law—everything is handled under rigid rules, and individual study and handling of children cannot be had."

IN FIRST DEGREE

The Niccolls boy was convicted of murder in the first degree and sent to the penitentiary for life. Subsequent efforts failed to have him paroled to Father Flanagan's famous boys' industrial farm in Nebraska. There, child welfare groups held, he could have been educated and prepared for life under a selfhelp and discipline program that has redeemed and sent back into society, as safe citizens, scores of boys who otherwise would have been criminals.

Herbert Niccolls killed John L. Wormell, sheriff, at Asotin, Wash. when the peace officer discovered him while he was hiding in a store at night, allegedly to burglarize the place.

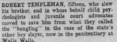

Herbert Nicholls case. *1933*

Father Flanagan (fourth from right) and his brother Father Patrick (second from left) on a fishing trip to Idaho. *1945*

Symbolic kickoff for the Boys Town vs. Detroit Catholic Central football game. *1944*

With Patrick Okura. *1946*

Selling war bonds in the Boys Town gift shop. *1943*

Alumnus Wesley Haggard and Father Flanagan. Haggard was awarded the Silver Star for bravery during World War II. *1944*

Talking with Irish children in Ennis, County Clare, Ireland. *1946*

Speaking to the children of his home town Ballymoe, Ireland. *1946*

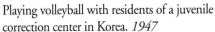
Playing volleyball with residents of a juvenile correction center in Korea. *1947*

On his arrival in Tokyo, Father Flanagan's plane suffered two flat tires after a braking problem. *1947*

Reviewing the living conditions of war orphans in Korea. *1947*

Visiting with residents of
the GYA Girls Center,
Heidelberg, Germany. *1948*

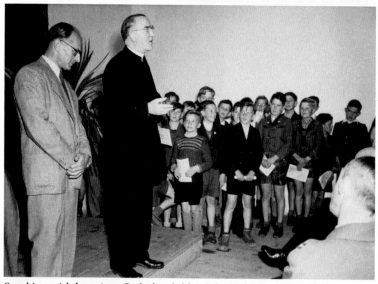

Speaking with boys in a Catholic children's home in Salzburg, Austria. *1948*

Last photograph taken of Father Flanagan prior to his death. Berlin. *1948*

A crowd of 1,500 people, including the residents of Boys Town, gathers at the Omaha Municipal Airport when Father Flanagan's remains are returned to America. *1948*

Residents of Boys Town pray before Father Flanagan's casket. *1948*

Father Patrick Flanagan blesses the casket of his brother Father Edward Flanagan. *1948*

President Harry Truman lays a wreath on the tomb of Father Flanagan. June 5, *1948*.

to find a system that would help prepare the boys for life after Boys Town, Father Flanagan, in autumn 1929, experimented with running his home like a military academy. He enlisted the services of Lt. John Scanlon, who had been the commandant of cadets at St. John's Military Academy in Los Angeles. The boys were organized into companies and all regulations were established along military lines including a military court to punish offenders. However, within a year, Scanlon was called back to Los Angeles and the military academy experiment soon faded.

In August 1929, Father Flanagan and forty boys traveled to West Branch, Iowa, to honor newly elected President Herbert Hoover. In a speech to the assembled crowd, Father Flanagan drew a connection between the new president and his homeless boys.

"Forty orphan boys come today to honor this spot, the birthplace fifty-five years ago of the orphan boy who now leads the nation. We pay tribute to Herbert Hoover's magnificent rise from obscurity. An orphan, deprived in early youth of life's dearest companions, has become President of the United States.

"The story of Herbert Hoover's life has a profound message for America. It beckons to America that it must not be inattentive to its unfortunate young. It is a forceful reminder that tucked away in an orphan mind may be the genius to guide the destinies of a great nation, that hidden in an orphan heart may be the surging humanitarian to feed and nourish a war-wrecked and desolate world.

"No one can tell from whence a great leader of the future will spring, from what remote or obscure beginning a young character will flower into manhood that will be the moving spirit of the community in which he lives...

"Hope is a great factor in bringing to the poor unfortunate orphan the lesson that he can overcome the obstacles which more fortunate boys do not have. We must plant hope in the heart of every orphan and homeless boy.[26]

Hope, and its opposite, despair, were emotions that Father Flanagan knew well. He saw them every week in the faces of the boys who came to Boys Town for help, but had to be turned away because he had no room. He turned away 185 boys in 1929.

In an essay in *Father Flanagan's Boys' Home Journal* titled "Homes or Jails," he wrote that the American people must face facts and make choices. "We who are not in the shadows of these misfortunes cannot realize how terrible it is to be forced to turn away homeless and helpless children. Each and every one of them is entitled to a chance to make good in life. It is not their fault that life has deprived them of everything that is near and dear, and essential to childhood. It is not their fault that a preoccupied world has no time to bother with orphaned and neglected children…

"It is estimated there are thousands upon thousands of homeless children in our country who are not being cared for, and who must look on the streets for the means of existence. These boys are our responsibilities whether or not we are willing to consider them such. We have no choice in the matter. Either we build homes for them now, or jails for them a little later."[27]

Father Flanagan wrote that it was less expensive to invest in homes for homeless children now, than to lose large sums to theft and destruction when these children turned to crime in order to survive. It was far less expensive to run an orphanage than a jail.

"Let our sociologists and criminologists prate about the causes of crime; let them deplore poverty, drunkenness, unemployment, irreligion, and the other innumerable factors that are the causes of crime. Why do they not go to the ultimate root of all these causes, and look to the neglected childhood of the nation in which exists the germ of nearly all crime?

"… Our Home is but the instrument in the hands of the American people. Whether or not the boy of today becomes the useful man or the destructive criminal of tomorrow depends on their answer to the question: Shall we build and support homes for these neglected boys, or shall we erect jails and penitentiaries for them after they become hardened and incurable criminals?"[28]

Father Flanagan needed more room, so he could take in more boys and change more lives. His new building program would do just that. Unfortunately, Father Flanagan and his boys would face setbacks along the way. The first occurred on Sunday morning, March, 2, 1930.

One of Boys Town's farm workers was backing a tractor out of the storage shed when the fuel tank suddenly exploded, spraying flaming gasoline in all directions. The driver made it out safely, but the shed was soon engulfed in flames. Hearing the explosion, W.J. Murphy, the farm superintendent, ran from the cow barn about a hundred yards away. The eight boys working with him ran to investigate as well. By the time they arrived, the flames, fanned by a stiff wind, had spread to the walls of the power house.

Murphy grabbed a water hose and began to fight the fire and the boys ran to the nearby horse barn to save the trapped animals. Boys were arriving from all directions, but the smoke was so thick and the flames so hot that Murphy waved them back. Seventeen-year-old Adolph Lopez ignored the command and dashed into the flaming power house. He located the main power switch and cut off electricity to the power lines that fed Boys Town. He emerged coughing and singed, but unharmed.

Eventually, six fire trucks from the Omaha Fire Department placed the fire under control. The granary and horse barn were destroyed and much farm equipment was lost. The power house, which contained the laundry, tailor shop and clothing storerooms, was gutted. The heating plant had been saved by Lopez's quick action. The boilers were undamaged.

The ruins were still smoldering when hundreds of people from Omaha and other nearby towns began to arrive with clothing and bedding to replace what had been lost in the fire. Newspapers and radio stations combined to publicize the tragedy and offers of help poured in from throughout the country.[29]

The home had insurance, but it didn't cover all of the losses, which were estimated at about $50,000. Father Flanagan used the fire as the focus of a new fundraising campaign. The result: three new buildings were dedicated in October of 1930.

The fire was not the only tragedy that Father Flanagan faced in 1930. In June, an infection began in Michael Flanagan's inner ear and spread to other parts of his skull. Father Flanagan's younger brother succumbed to mastoiditis at age thirty-six.

He had a beautiful tenor voice and sang in many area choirs. "In his heart," Father Flanagan wrote, "he felt and meant what he sang – his singing was the expression of his soul, sincere and noble."[30] The funeral had to be held in Omaha's St. Cecelia Cathedral to accommodate the large crowd of mourners. The coffin was carried out to the sound of the Father Flanagan Celebrity Choir singing one of Michael Flanagan's favorite songs, "Goin' Home."[31]

Despite his personal tragedies, 1930 was a successful year for Father Flanagan. His building expansion had been completed, and 742 boys had applied for entrance to Boys Town, but only 169 were admitted. Some had been turned away because they did not fall between the ages of twelve and sixteen, the age limits of the Home. "One woman, who had six children ranging from six months to nine years was insistent that we take all of them," Flanagan wrote. "We refused because of their age, but she tried to bargain with us by keeping the six-month-old." Others were refused because they were too old. "An anxious mother desired to place her youngest son in our care," Flanagan wrote. "He had taken to drinking but she knew we could help him. He was 22 years old." Boys Town now had boys from every state in the union, thirty-five to forty different nationalities and every race.[32]

The year ended on a positive note for Father Flanagan when he was named "Omaha's Most Valuable Citizen for 1930" by the American Legion Post Number One. In a ceremony held in May of 1931, Flanagan was honored by a host of prominent Omahans. When he returned to Boys Town, each boy lined up to shake his hand in congratulations. They were also saying goodbye.[33]

Father Flanagan's health never had been strong. His long hours and constant worry about the survival of his Home had taken their toll. He was ordered by his doctor to take six months of uninterrupted rest and recuperation. The building expansion of 1930 had just been completed and Boys Town was running smoothly, but Father Flanagan was afraid that the slightest mistake might bring about a complete collapse of everything for which he had worked. He argued with his doctor for hours, but in the end his physician received Father Flanagan's promise to take the six-month rest at a sanitarium in Denver, Colorado.

The next challenge was to find someone who could continue the work of the Home in Father Flanagan's absence. As he had done so many times in the past, he went to his family for help. His older brother, Father Patrick Flanagan, agreed to oversee the Home while his brother was recovering his health. There would still be a Father Flanagan in charge at Boys Town.[34]

While Father Edward Flanagan settled into life at the sanitarium, hundreds of miles to the west, Hubert Niccols found a gun. He was twelve years old in August 1931. For many years, his father had been an inmate at a hospital for the insane. His mother had come in and out of his life, abandoning him three times. Eventually, he was placed in the custody of his grandmother who was frail and unable to control her grandson. Hubert roamed the streets and did what he wanted. He was dirty, he was hungry and, now, he was armed.

The gun was a toy to Hubert. He had seen his heroes use guns in the Westerns and gangster shows at the local movie theater. He kept it in his pocket as he walked along the darkening streets of his town. It gave him a feeling of power. No one stopped him or asked what he was doing out so late at night.

It had been fifteen hours since he had eaten, and he was hungry. He knew the local grocery store was nearby. The store was dark, but a window had been left unlocked and Hubert squirmed through, knocking over a pyramid of cans as he hit the floor.

The sheriff was passing by, making his rounds, when he heard the cans tumble. He stopped to investigate the noise. Hubert ducked behind a barrel as the law enforcement officer entered the store. Silhouetted in the doorframe, he moved toward Hubert. This was just like in the movies. Hubert grabbed his gun, pointed it at the shadowy figure and pulled the trigger.

Outside, there were shouts and the sounds of people running. The door was pushed all the way open and the lights flashed on. Hubert stood in the light, still holding the gun. Someone snatched it away and threw him against the counter. They checked the sheriff for a pulse, but he was dead.

"Why did you kill the sheriff?"

"I was just playing, like in the movies," Hubert replied.[35]

The case became a national sensation. Hubert's mother was located and she was expected to plead for her son. She declared she wasn't interested in him anymore. The trial moved quickly. The evidence seemed overwhelming.

Hubert didn't really understand what he had done or why he was on trial. The court proceedings bored him and, while the jury was deliberating, he fell asleep. When the jury returned, the judge ordered the defendant be awakened to hear its verdict. Hubert was told to stand and face the jury. He was found guilty of murder in the first degree and sentenced to life in prison at the Washington State penitentiary.[36]

Washington state law prohibited juveniles from being incarcerated with adults, yet juveniles convicted of capital offenses could not be housed in a juvenile penal institution. The solution was to put twelve-year-old Hubert Niccols in solitary confinement.[37]

In October of 1931, Father Flanagan received a telegram from a friend telling him about the Niccols' case. He sent a letter to Washington letting the court know that if the state didn't have a suitable institution to house Hubert, he was willing to take him at Boys Town. The return letter he received from the court did not satisfy him. Ignoring his doctor's orders, he left the sanitarium and began a campaign to get custody of Hubert Niccols.

He contacted the newspapers with his offer to help the boy. He asked his radio listeners to write to the governor on his behalf. "Letters and wires, resolutions and protests were filed by veterans' organizations, women's clubs, parent teacher groups and others throughout the country."[38]

Father Flanagan traveled to Washington State and met with many of its prominent citizens at a meeting designed to find a solution to the case. A telegram from the governor was read welcoming Father Flanagan to Washington. He was encouraged by his reception. "I addressed those at the banquet on my work with homeless and abandoned boys, and told them that thousands of such boys were being neglected today all over our great country with no one to care much whether they lived or died or spent their days behind bars. It took a Hubert Niccols, by his material act of murder, to awaken an indifferent society to the real condition of neglect of these unloved and unwanted boys, who of themselves are so helpless, unattractive and insignificant that their appeal for bread and love go unanswered."[39]

On November 22, 1931, he met with Gov. Roland Hartley. The meeting was cordial and the governor told Father Flanagan he would speak to the parole board and give him his final decision soon. Encouraged, but exhausted by his efforts, Father Flanagan immediately discontinued his efforts on behalf of Hubert Niccols and belatedly followed his doctor's advice by leaving for California and a well-deserved rest.[40]

One month later, Father Flanagan received his answer from the governor. It was a lengthy letter that read in part, "… Because of the youth of this boy, his case attracted nationwide attention and furnished opportunity for sensational newspapers to wring the heartstrings of highly emotional and sympathetic people…

"… In my opinion, nothing in recent years has taken place so detrimental to the youth of our land as the melodramatic publicity and exploitation which attended your trip to Washington and the request to have this boy turned over to your institution…

"… I am deeply impressed by the sincere sympathy that has prompted many of our people in their concern for the well-being of this lad. Let me assure these a well-ordered routine fills his days, embracing all activities necessary to fully develop him, even excelling the opportunities of many boys on the outside…

"… According to expert testimony which is well corroborated by the boy's history, he is at present unsafe to be at large. This case is the responsibility of the State of Washington. The Chief Executive would be derelict in his duty should he undertake to transfer the responsibility to an agency in another state. In view of all these facts, your request for the parole of this boy cannot be considered."[41]

The governor had made it plain he believed that not only was this young boy enjoying benefits not available to other youths his age, but that Father Flanagan's motivation in the case was purely one of "melodramatic publicity and exploitation."

In a letter published in the *Boys' Home Journal*, the governor's motives were questioned. He was accused of "cheap gutter politics" for claiming Flanagan's only motivation in the case was publicity, while, "…he [the governor] has reprinted thousands of copies of his letter to you and mailed them throughout the state, at state expense, in order to get more votes for the next election…

"… Governor Hartley may be right in keeping Hubert Niccols behind prison walls. I don't think so, but regardless of that fact, he had no right to attack you, and, if you were not a

Catholic priest, I would tell you to take off your coat and give him the physical beating such a politician deserves."[42]

The case dragged on throughout 1932 as the two men exchanged letters. Despite public pressure, the governor would not yield. The governor was not re-elected, in part because of the Niccols case, but the new administration kept the boy imprisoned. In time, the public lost interest and moved on to other stories, but Father Flanagan kept up his correspondence. In 1940, nine years after the initial sentence, a new governor granted Hubert Niccols his parole.

In August 1932, the *Boys' Home Journal* reported that the Home was perilously near to closing due, in part, to the effects of the Great Depression. Unemployment was at an all-time high and more and more homeless boys sought refuge at Boys Town. Some, such as Arthur and Franklin Yoder, traveled long distances to get to Boys Town. The Yoder brothers walked three hundred miles from Sedalia, Missouri, north to Boys Town. It took them six weeks.[43]

In November of 1932, presidential candidate Franklin Roosevelt and his wife, Eleanor, toured Boys Town, declaring it to be "one of the most beautiful places" visited on their cross-country trip."[44] The Great Depression was tightening its grip on the country and, soon, climatic change was going to make things worse.

The early to mid 1930s were the height of the Dust Bowl years in Nebraska. In August 1933, the boys formed water bucket brigades to try to save their vegetable gardens. While some crops survived, the drought destroyed the oat crop, nineteen acres of potatoes and a hundred acres of corn. Another year of drought followed in 1934 when 320 acres of crops and vegetables burned.[45]

By the end of 1934, Boys Town had housed 3,478 boys, since its founding in 1917. There were 200 boys currently in residence. There had been applications from 407 boys in 1934, but there was only room for 184. As boys were placed with adoptive families or graduated, their spots were quickly filled.[46]

In an effort to make Boys Town an official municipality, Father Flanagan petitioned the government to establish a post office at Boys Town, Nebraska. In November 1934, the Postmaster General granted Flanagan's petition and a post office was established with Patrick Norton as its first postmaster.

Before Boys Town had its own post office, Al Witcofski and Father Flanagan would drive to Omaha's main post office to collect their mail. Parking was often difficult, so the pair would park in the back of the building.

"One night," Witcofski recalled, "we came out and the car was gone. So we got a cab and went down to the police station. 'Ya, it's here.' It was two dollars or something. So we paid the two dollars. Well the next night we went down and the same darn thing. We ran into old Paul Sutton, who was the head of the detective department. And he said, 'What are you doing here, Father?' Father said, 'towed my car in again.'"

Witcofski said Sutton then asked Father Flanagan if that meant his car had been towed the night before as well, and Father Flanagan replied that it had. Sutton told one of the men at the desk to give Father Flanagan his money back and then the officer asked for Father Flanagan's license plate number. From then on, according to Witcofski, "He could park the darn thing in the middle of the street and no one would ever bother it."[47]

The first two weeks of 1935 were exciting times at Boys Town. For the first time since the short-lived experiment with self-government in 1926, Boys Town was going to hold an election. When Boys Town was officially placed on the map, with the chartering of a post office by the federal government, it was decided that, like all other municipalities, it must have elected officials.

Two political parties, "Help Our Town" and "Build Boys Town" quickly formed. Two weeks of vigorous campaigning followed. The election was held on January 15, 1935. "Shortly after 7:30 in the evening all the boys gathered in the new gymnasium building. At the far end of the auditorium three booths had been set up on the stage. In an orderly line, the 200 boys filed up… Adherents of the two factions were permitted within almost shouting distance of the polling places that they might better display painted placards. To these they added their lusty shouts as each boy approached the ballot box. The band lent an air of authentic campaign atmosphere to the scene with its contribution of martial music."[48]

Tony Villone was elected the first official mayor of Boys Town. In a short victory address he stated, "Boys, we'll never back down on our election program. The Build Boys Town party is going to work hard to carry out every promise it made."[49]

On August 4, 1936, the county commissioners of Douglas County, Nebraska, officially authorized the incorporation of the village of Boys Town. It was now listed on road maps and on state documents as an official village. Outside the entrance to Birch Drive, on the road leading to the highway, a sign was erected. It read: "Boy Town – population – 275."

CHAPTER
7

Welcoming Hollywood

BOYS TOWN HAD BEEN HOME to wayward boys for nearly twenty years and Father Flanagan had justly earned a national reputation as a spokesman for troubled youths. His reputation led Roy Helgensen, city editor for the *Washington Herald*, to telegraph Flanagan about a Washington D.C. case that he thought might interest him.

"Judge Fay L. Bentley, juvenile court, has sentenced two 15 yr. old average boys of good families to 6 years each in a reformatory for taking an automobile, trial lasted 2 minutes and was held in secret. Youths, parents and other witnesses were given no opportunity to testify. Boys had never been arrested before."[1]

The judge, a former truant officer, had interpreted the boys' citation for two days of truancy, in 1931, as a criminal act, allowing her to assess a harsher punishment for the car theft. Helgensen wrote that Bentley was being strongly criticized for her action by prominent citizens and the local media. Congressional impeachment action had been threatened. He wired that he thought Flanagan's opinion of the sentence was important and urged him to respond to the paper as soon as possible.[2]

Father Flanagan was quick to reply, sending a letter to the newspaper, the same day he received the telegram. "…While I have always upheld, with the greatest respect, the rulings of courts and judges sitting on the bench, this ruling of Judge Bentley has aroused me to condemn this woman juvenile court judge and look upon her action as one that will aid and abet crime and criminals. Her marathon trial and conviction of two young boys, 15 years of age, to six years in a juvenile prison, for taking an automobile, all within two minutes, without any witnesses, parents, or legal advice for the youngsters, who are first offenders, should cause all respectable and respected judges of the courts of our land to bow their heads in shame and apology for such an erratic, unripe, unjust and illegal procedure on the part of a sworn defender of the rights of our citizens."[3]

Flanagan's compassion for the boys and anger at the judge are clear – not only from the speed of his reply, but from his tendency to write long sentences, punctuated with several commas, when he was passionate about a subject.

"I am not an upholder of the delinquent," Flanagan continued, "even the first offender type. He must be punished and taught a lesson that he will remember, but a lesson that will teach, not embitter him against society… These young men, embittered, will come forth from this prison at the age of 21 with a living hate of all law, all judges and all courts, and will become apt and willing members of our criminal population. Had Judge Bentley placed two guns in the hands of her two convicts and sent them out to join the ranks of the criminal, she would have done less harm to them and to society as sending them to a juvenile prison for their first offence to give them a thorough training in the ways of crime."[4]

Despite requests for his advice and involvement on national issues, Father Flanagan never let his attention stray

too far from his Home for boys. His boys always came first –
no matter how important or how trivial the matter. In June of
1937, Boys Town graduated its first high school class of ten
students. The class included Wesley Haggard, who would go
on to fame as a war hero at Guadalcanal, and Boys Town's first
boy mayor, Tony Villone. Just one month later, Father Flanagan
had his own celebration as he observed the silver jubilee of his
ordination as a priest.

Father Flanagan's desire to construct all of his buildings
from brick and stone was reinforced by two fires that occurred
in 1937. The first began just after midnight on August 1. A
ferocious Midwestern thunderstorm rumbled across the Boys
Town campus and woke most of the boys with its flashes of
lightning and peals of thunder. As they watched its progress,
a small flicker of fire appeared on the roof of the main barn.
It had been struck by lightning and within a few minutes the
entire roof was engulfed in flames.

The boys rushed down the stairs of their dormitory, prepared to do what they could to battle the fire, but they were
stopped at the door by the adult staff and some of the older
boys. They were told it was too dangerous and they would only
be in the way. By the time the fire trucks arrived from Omaha, the barn was lost. It had contained thirty-nine tons of hay
and four tons of straw, "which burned with such intense heat
that window glass melted like sugar candy and dripped to the
ground."[5] All of the animals had been taken safely away, but
some valuable farm machinery was destroyed.

As he had previously, Father Flanagan used the disaster as
an opportunity to raise money for construction of more permanent buildings. The story on the fire, in the September 1937 issue of the *Boys' Home Journal*, featured a clip-out coupon to be
sent back to the home with a donation for new construction.[6]

Just a few months later, on November 2, 1937, a second fire broke out in the only remaining wooden building on campus. In addition to a hundred tons of straw, recently purchased for winter feed, all of the boys' spare clothing had been stored in the building. The fire burned for more than twelve hours until nothing was left but ashes.

Father Flanagan called in his architects, and the Board of Directors gave its approval for the new buildings. They broke ground on the new farm buildings in May and they were completed and in use by autumn 1938.[7]

On October 23, 1937, Father Flanagan was appointed a "Right Reverend Monsignor" by Pope Pius XI. There was a colorful ceremony, held in the Boys Town auditorium a month later, celebrating Flanagan's elevation to monsignor. Many prominent citizens, including Omaha's Bishop James Ryan, attended the ceremony.

Of course, all of Boys Town's citizens attended as well. "It was all very interesting. The boys listened in respectful silence. Afterwards they came to Father, and stammered in various pronunciations his new title, 'Monsignor.' Father smiled, a sweet and understanding smile, and then asked his boys, one and all to keep in mind that to them he would always be just plain 'Father Flanagan.' This is the way Father wanted it, that is how it had been down through the years. No boy in his home would ever dream of addressing him as other than 'Father Flanagan.'"[8]

Perhaps the proudest member of the audience at his elevation to monsignor was his mother, Nora Flanagan. Ever since he was a small boy in Ballymoe, Father Flanagan had been comforted by his mother's presence. She had long been an inspiration to him and many of her teachings had laid the foundation for his lifelong philosophies about his fellow man.

Now ninety-two years old, she no longer lived at Boys Town, but stayed with her daughter, Susan Dwyer, in nearby Omaha. On Sunday morning, March 20, 1938, Nora Flanagan attended Mass at St. Cecilia's Cathedral. Afterward, she returned to Dwyer's home and insisted on helping about the house in the afternoon. That evening, Father Patrick Flanagan stopped by to visit his mother. While he was at the house, his mother suffered a heart attack and her son gave her the last rites of the Catholic Church. According to Willets, "She smiled reassuringly at those about her and breathed her last."[9]

Three days later, her sons, Fathers Patrick and Edward Flanagan, celebrated a Solemn Requiem High Mass that was attended by Bishop Ryan and fifty-six priests. Members of the Holy Rosary Sodality formed a lane of honor at the funeral procession.

While Father Flanagan mourned his mother's passing, Hollywood producer John Considine was outlining his idea for a movie about a home for boys. Considine contacted Father Flanagan and the two began exchanging letters about the project. They reached a preliminary agreement, and Considine dispatched two men to Boys Town to gather material for a screenplay.[10]

Five months passed before Father Flanagan heard anything more from Hollywood. In mid-December, a letter arrived from Metro-Goldwyn-Mayer. Considine explained that after several writers made unsuccessful attempts at writing a movie script about Boys Town, Dore Schary had been selected as the primary scriptwriter for the movie.

In a run-through of sorts, a few weeks before the movie

Boys Town began production, a documentary titled, *The City of Little Men,* was filmed. The documentary, which provided a behind-the-scenes look at life at Boys Town, was to be used for educational and fundraising purposes.

According to a story in the *Boys' Home Journal,* director J. Walter Ruben and writer Schary, were then sent "…here to get the feel of Boys Town so that their dramatization would be true to life." Both men were impressed with Boys Town's youngest citizen, seven-year-old Andy Cain, and thought he would be perfect to play the character of Pee Wee in the movie. "They were also enthusiastic over the a cappella choir, declared it a splendidly trained organization and a good part for the choir has been written into the picture."[11]

The two men spent several days taking pictures and interviewing Boys Town residents for stories about Father Flanagan and his home. On their last night, they hosted an ice cream social for the boys. They told the boys that Spencer Tracy was to play Father Flanagan and Mickey Rooney was to star as "Whitey." Best of all, many of the movie's scenes were to be shot at Boys Town and some boys might get bit parts in the movie with everyone else acting as extras in the crowd scenes.[12]

Prompted by Ruben and Schary's enthusiastic endorsement, Father Flanagan took Andy and Jimmie Cain to Hollywood to screen test for the role of Pee Wee. Neither boy did well in the screen test, but both were promised bit parts in the movie. Eventually a young actor named Bobs Watson was chosen to play the part of Pee Wee.[13]

The final script for *Boys Town,* based on an original screenplay by Eleanor Griffin and Dore Schary, was submitted to Father Flanagan in May 1938. Father Flanagan received approval of the script from the church hierarchy and notified Hollywood that all was well. Several weeks later, a crew of fifty-eight left

Hollywood and traveled to Omaha to begin shooting the movie.

Kathryn Dwyer, Father Flanagan's fifteen-year-old niece, was present during the two weeks of filming and wrote of her impressions in detail in an article she titled, "Boys Town Looks at Hollywood." She told her story through the eyes of a boy with whom she had talked each day while the movie was being made.

"Up the driveway they came…ten cabs full of them. Oaf and Slim and I were on Post Office duty every morning during the summer, so we couldn't stand out in front and cheer with the rest of the kids as the Hollywood troupe entered Boys Town. We sure yelled from the window, though, and we didn't miss seeing anything either. Hollywood hung out of the windows and yelled and waved back. Everyone was terribly excited. The cabs stopped one by one in front of the office building and pretty soon lots of people were milling around all over the place. The Postmistress, not getting any work out of us anyway, said we could go for 10 minutes. Boy, we sure shoved out of there in a hurry!

"Just then a cab drove up and Mickey, Spencer Tracy and a fat man got out. We had met Mickey and Spencer the day before, but this was the grand opening so we made as much noise as we could. Mickey yelled back at us and shook hands with as many of the kids as he could before the fat man dragged him over to Father Flanagan.

"…The first chance we had Slim and I set out to get the dope on Mickey Rooney. He was lying under a tree waiting to shoot a scene with Bobs Watson, Pee-Wee in the movie. When he saw us, he gave us the sign to come over. Slim, who can talk anyone into a sore throat, found his match in Mickey."[14]

The movie crew took over the village and everything ran

on its schedule for a few weeks. Weather often determined the shooting schedule and the shooting schedule determined everything else at Boys Town. The movie was shot during July, which meant the actors and crew also had to put up with humidity and heat. In order to get the lighting or the colors just right, Director Norman Taurog (who had replaced the original director, J. Walter Ruben) had to make many last-minute scene adjustments.

"It took us about a week to get used to everything topsy-turvy. If they weren't painting our sidewalks brown, they were throwing dirt all over them. Bells rang continually at the wrong time. The outdoor clock on the office building was changed every time they shot an outdoor scene and Father was worn out from ducking out of sight as they took shots of his office. Things were in a continual uproar. We were late for meals, forgot to do our chores and altogether life was a circus... All Father Flanagan said was that we should have as good a time as possible without getting in the way."[15]

"One really swell scene that we did get in one was the one in which Pee-Wee is run over. They shot that in the morning too, down on the highway. In the picture, it comes just after Mickey starts to run away from Boys Town and Pee-Wee goes down the driveway after him. As he runs across the highway, a truck comes zooming down and hits him. It was the hardest scene of all, they said, because they certainly couldn't afford to have Pee-Wee hurt. In fact, they brought a stunt driver all the way from Hollywood to make sure nothing would happen. He was to drive the truck just up to Pee-Wee and then jam on the brakes real fast. And Pee-Wee was supposed to fall down like he's been hit. In the end, they were afraid to even take that risk, so this is what they did. They began the scene with Pee-Wee already run over, and the truck right up next to him. Then carefully they did everything backwards. The truck backed up and Pee-Wee got up and stood in position. Afterwards the cameraman showed the scene in reverse action and it looked like the real McCoy."[16]

Father Flanagan hosted a barbecue for movie crew members on the night before they left. Anticipation grew as the days passed because no one knew if the movie would be successful or what effect it might have on the fortunes of Boys Town. They could only wait for the film's completion.

The world premiere of *Boys Town* was to be held at the Omaha Theatre on September 7, 1938. Hollywood celebrities Spencer Tracy, Mickey Rooney and Maureen O'Sullivan arrived by train with Father Flanagan. The day of the premiere, school was suspended at Boys Town and the movie's producer, John Considine, brought out a truckload of ice cream, candy and cookies for a party with the boys.

More than twenty thousand people jammed the streets around the theater as the time for the movie premiere approached. Spotlights swept across the Omaha skyline and could be seen for miles into the countryside. Special traffic squads were needed to handle the press of the crowd as the celebrities arrived. In addition to the Hollywood stars, Omaha's mayor, Dan Butler, Nebraska's governor, Roy Cochran, Bishop James Ryan, and Father Flanagan's old friends Henry Monsky and Francis Matthews attended and gave brief comments about Father Flanagan's work.[17]

The movie proved to be popular wherever it was shown and broke several box office records. It made Father Flanagan an international celebrity and the demand for him on the lecture circuit increased dramatically. He used his celebrity to expound on his ideas for solving the problems of juvenile delinquency.[18]

The movie's success also brought some unintended consequences. Rumors about vast sums of money paid to Father Flanagan for the movie rights swept the country and caused a significant decline in fundraising. The October issue of Boys Town's newspaper, now renamed the *Boys Town Times*, used its front page to talk about the movie premiere and also to clear up some misconceptions.

"Boys Town received five thousand dollars for the movie rights. There is no other arrangement for royalties or further payment of any kind and the five thousand dollars already paid has been, almost in its entirety, used up in expenses in connection with the making of the picture.

"Father Flanagan has asked the *Times* to say that while he is happy that the picture has been made and that he feels that it will be invaluable to him in bringing his work before the eyes of the public, yet to let such rumors persist would do more damage than the picture could ever do good."[19]

One of Father Flanagan's first appearances following the movie premiere was as the featured speaker at the National Council of Catholic Charities, held in Richmond, Virginia, in October 1938. The topic was "Institutional Care of Behavior Problem Boys."

He used the opportunity to hammer home his opinions on the root causes of behavior problems in boys, claiming the home, the Church and the school system had all evaded their responsibility in properly caring for these boys.

"Such boys have been robbed of character developing factors which would insure healthy normal citizens. The breaking down of the modern home, the laziness, selfishness, ignorance and downright viciousness of too many parents, lie at the root of the delinquency problem.

"There are certain fundamental needs beyond those of food, growth and shelter, which are vital to mental and moral health at all ages. The denial of any of them leads to an unbalanced organization of the individual and results in a twisted character. Human beings of all ages need recognition, security, approval, and the thrill of achievement. The quest for the fulfillment of these natural urges is the motivating factor in all human endeavor."[20]

In a December 1938 speech before the Calvert Club in Washington D.C., Father Flanagan showed the film, *The City of Little Men*, and spoke out against reform schools. The crowd of congressmen, diplomats, university presidents, prominent businessmen and clergy heard Flanagan condemn the school system of rehabilitation. "Everyone knows the reform school system is wrong," Father Flanagan told the audience. "Then why is there absolutely nothing done to change it? We have good men in these schools, but the system is wrong. You cannot help a boy by putting him behind bars."[21] While in Washington, Father Flanagan also met with President Franklin D. Roosevelt and discussed the problems of juvenile delinquency on a national scale. Roosevelt would call on Father Flanagan for advice on this subject many times in the years to come.

The 1939 Academy Awards held special meaning for Father Flanagan and Boys Town. Dore Schary and Eleanor Griffin won an Oscar for best original screenplay and Spencer Tracy was named Best Actor for his portrayal of Father Flanagan. In his acceptance speech, Tracy gave full credit to Father Flanagan, saying his impersonation of the priest was believable because of the time he spent at Boys Town. In response to a congratulatory message from Father Flanagan, Tracy wrote, "Thank you so much for your nice message. The credit is due you and I am glad we got it for the sake of Boys Town. Very best wishes – Spencer Tracy."[22]

On the evening of the Academy Award Dinner, Father Flanagan lay sick in bed with a bad cold. Two days later, Father Flanagan was still bedridden when a heavy parcel arrived from California. When he opened the package, Father Flanagan found Tracy's Oscar statuette. Inscribed on the base of the Oscar were the following words: "To Father Edward J. Flanagan, whose great human qualities, kindly simplicity and inspiring courage were strong enough to shine through my humble efforts."[23] It was a magnanimous gesture by Tracy and cemented the friendship that had grown between the two men. They remained good friends for the rest of Father Flanagan's life. The Oscar still resides in Boys Town and the statuette is prominently displayed in the Boys Town Hall of History.

The movie continued to garner attention around the world, including showings in the Vatican and in Father Flanagan's homeland of Ireland. A showing in Dublin attracted "unprecedented crowds, including hundreds of Father Flanagan's closest friends." In time, the movie even made its way to Castlerea, near Father Flanagan's home town of Ballymoe, where it was seen by his sister Kate Staunton. "In many towns throughout Ireland arrangements were made to display the picture out-of-doors when no suitable auditorium was available."[24]

The movie, *Boys Town*, was attracting attention from more than just movie fans. More homeless boys sought admittance and Father Flanagan had to turn far too many away. In 1938, 1,341 boys applied for admission to Boys Town. The vast majority, 1,207 boys, was told there was no room.[25] Overcrowding had been a problem for years and Father Flanagan was determined to create room for more boys. In March 1939, he announced an ambitious expansion plan that would cost $635,000. He planned to build four new dormitories, each housing 125 boys, as well as a new dining hall where they all could be fed. This new construction would allow him to take in 500 boys. The Board of Trustees, headed by Bishop James Ryan, approved the plan and fundraising began immediately.[26]

On April 25, 1939, ground was broken for the new dormitories and the dining hall. One of the dormitory buildings was paid for entirely by a national fundraising campaign sponsored by the Fraternal Order of Eagles.[27]

One of the millions who watched the movie was Mary Dowd from New York City. She saw it over and over again, taking friends and relatives each time she watched it. She wrote Father Flanagan telling him of her interest to do something to help his boys. On one of his trips to New York, Father Flanagan met with Dowd and her attorney. That June, Dowd traveled to Boys Town and met with Flanagan and Bishop Ryan. She attended a Mass being celebrated by the Rev. Henry Sutti in the little chapel of the main school building. Sutti was the first Boys Town graduate to be ordained into the priesthood.[28]

Dowd was so impressed by her visit that she agreed to fund a church, formally named The Immaculate Conception of the Blessed Virgin Mary, but informally called Dowd Chapel. It was to be dedicated to the memory of her parents and siblings. Construction began in October 1939 and was completed in January 1941.[29]

His boys now had a magnificent place to worship, and Father Flanagan turned his attention to finding help in educating his young boys. He called on the Christian Brothers religious order. The necessary arrangements were made and in August

1939, the Brothers arrived. They taught first in the high school, but later worked in the grade school as well. Eventually, the Brothers assumed full responsibility for the entire Boys Town school system.[30] Father Flanagan became dissatisfied with their work, however, and terminated his contract with the Christian Brothers six years later.

The overwhelming success of *Boys Town* earned a fortune for Metro-Goldwyn-Mayer and talk of a sequel began almost immediately. At first, Father Flanagan hesitated to give approval to the project. In April 1939, with the promise of more money to help fund his expansion plans, he signed an agreement to shoot the sequel.

The *Boys Town Times* of February 23, 1940, featured a story on the new movie. In contrast to the $5,000 Father Flanagan was paid for the first movie, this time MGM agreed to pay Flanagan $100,000 for the movie rights, "...which will be applied against its present half a million dollar debt incurred for new buildings to take care of 500 homeless boys."[31] It was to be called *Men of Boys Town*, and Spencer Tracy and Mickey Rooney would reprise their roles.

The film was set in a boys' reformatory staffed by sadistic guards. Ironically, Father Flanagan was soon to become involved in a real-life situation that mirrored and exceeded the horrors portrayed in the film. *Men of Boys Town*, while a quality film, did not match the success of the original. It helped fund Father Flanagan's expansion effort and then faded into obscurity.[32] Just a few months after Father Flanagan signed the contract for *Men of Boys Town*, coverage of events at California's Whittier State School for Boys shocked the public, first in California and then throughout the nation.

Benny Moreno was thirteen years old when he hanged himself in the "Lost Privilege Cottage" at Whittier State School. He had been beaten and starved until he lost hope.

The inmates at Whittier reported that they were routinely lashed by the guards with leather whips, beaten, kicked and forced to "duck walk until they fell over."[33]

In response to Moreno's suicide, California's governor, Culbert L. Olson, asked for a report from Dr. Aaron J. Rosanoff, director of State Institutions. Rosanoff responded that Moreno was a "psychopathic personality" and therefore no blame for his death could be placed on school officials at Whittier.

The California Congress of Parents and Teachers was not satisfied by Rosanoff's report and demanded further inquiry. For several months, committee hearings were held, abuses were identified, but nothing changed. One year after Moreno's death, fifteen-year-old Edward Leiva was also found hanging from the ceiling in Whittier's Lost Privilege Cottage. Dr. Rosanoff's response was the same as before. Leiva was a "psychopathic personality" and the Whittier staff was blameless.[34]

R.A. Carrington, publisher of the *Los Angeles Examiner* newspaper, wrote to Father Flanagan and asked him to make a statement about the events at Whittier.

Father Flanagan's response was printed in the *Examiner* and reprinted in the *Boys Town Times*. In an essay titled "Suicide as an Escape from Brutality," he wrote: "In my opinion the system of all reform schools is wrong, basically wrong. The inmate looks upon his detention behind prison bars as a punishment and the program of rehabilitation is purely accidental if not indeed miraculous. A close analytical study of the State System will bear me out in the statement that punishment of the juvenile offender is the essential feature – the Alpha and Omega of the reform school's general program.

"… No need for me to try and describe the mental attitude of fear which grips the heart and mind of a boy who chooses suicide rather than submit to the punishment and brutality of guards. It must be one of the greatest moments of desperation – hopelessness, abandonment – the feeling that the unfortunate boy hasn't a friend in the world – save perhaps a mother, many miles away – but beyond his reach again.

"… He is branded in the very court that has been established to help him – a juvenile court – and sent to be a prey of a pack of human wolves who could grit their teeth and apply the lash to the unhappy victim who doesn't walk the chalked line.

"These boys do not need punishment – they need rehabilitation – just like a physically sick person needs medical and perhaps hospital care – these boys are mentally sick because they are starved of the principle vitamin in character development – love.

"… I have for the past 25 years condemned reform schools as unnecessary schools of torture and schools of crime… These reform schools do not reform. They turn out young fellows steeped in the poison of revenge – trained in the red lore of criminal anecdotes – young fellows with the determined resolve and the knowledge to seek vengeance on a society so stupid as to punish and not to cure."[35]

Public indignation about the events at Whittier prompted the governor to appoint a committee of citizens to investigate charges of brutality. After a three-month investigation, in December 1940, the committee issued a report calling for drastic changes in Whittier's administration. Within a month after the report was issued, two Whittier guards were convicted of charges of brutality and sentenced to less than a year in prison. Still the story would not go away and the governor decided to appoint a three-member commission to reform and reorganize California's institutions for delinquent minors. This commission was headed by Father Flanagan and included William B. Cox of the Osborne Society of New York and Helen Mellinkoff, a sociologist from Beverly Hills, California.[36]

The appointment of the commission was met with both hope and skepticism. While they applauded the governor's choice of committee members, the *San Francisco Examiner* editorialized: "The degree to which the commission is supported by State Officials will determine its success and the permanence thereof..."[37] Unfortunately, the newspaper's words proved prophetic.

Father Flanagan, accompanied by Patrick Norton and the commissioners traveled to California in early April 1941 and began an investigation of Whittier. They learned the institution had 232 inmates and 109 employees – one employee for every two inmates, most of the employees being political appointees.

One of the first things Father Flanagan did was to suspend E. J. Milne, superintendent of the Whittier School. Norton was appointed acting superintendent until the investigation was completed. Mellinkoff queried Dr. Rosanoff about Lost Privilege Cottage and charged that boys had been kept in solitary confinement there for five days, completely nude. In response to the accusations, Dr. Rosanoff blamed the Whittier staff and claimed that the Lost Privilege Cottage was a necessary evil.

In contrast, Los Angeles newspapers ran several articles that showed Father Flanagan with the boys from Whittier and praised him for the dramatic changes he had made in the school. On April 18, 1941, Father Flanagan's commission handed in its report to the governor. The report included a very specific program of reform that the commission believed could dramatically improve the lives of the boys at Whittier. They were thanked and all the commissioners returned home, at least temporarily. The commission also recommended that Cox be retained as the permanent superintendent of the Whittier School to ensure the reforms be carried out. The governor agreed.[38]

A few days after his return to California, Cox suspended his assistant superintendent, F. C. Van Velzer, a protégé of Milne, saying, "He appeared to be qualified only as a janitor!" This was too much for the entrenched political forces backing Milne and Van Velzer. When another boy attempted suicide, Cox was held responsible and forced to resign. In a letter to Dr. Rosanhoff, Cox wrote: "I am now fully convinced that I was brought to California under false pretenses and that there is not now and never has been any honest intention on your part or on the part of members of the personnel board to do aught else than practice political chicanery." Within a year, embittered and broken in health, Cox was dead.[39]

One of Milne's political allies wrote in triumph to Father Flanagan: "You believed you could turn one 'Evil and Godless' public school into a Roman Catholic religious school, which you have failed to do, even though Cox was sneaked in so quietly that no one knew he was there with a few exceptions, your contemptible attempt to force Dr. Rosanhoff to hail the temporary appointment of Cox as head of our State School, in a letter to the S.F. Examiner was an absolute failure, as was the movie – 'Men of Boys Town' – which was one of the most colossal failures in movie history."[40]

In time, Whittier returned to its old practices. In January 1944, stories of brutality at the school began to reappear in California newspapers. When told of the recurring events,

Father Flanagan said, "May God help these little children and give them hope in this dark day."[41]

Leaving California behind, Father Flanagan returned to Boys Town. He returned to spring planting and political elections. James Ross of Honolulu was elected mayor of Boys Town in May 1941. Seven months later, on December 8, Ross, along with every other boy in the senior class, lined up outside Father Flanagan's door. Each wanted to volunteer for the Armed Services of the United States of America. They wanted to serve their country during a very desperate time.

8

America's No. One War Dad

IT WAS EARLY SUNDAY AFTERNOON when the news about an attack on Pearl Harbor first reached Boys Town. A basketball game was abandoned as the boys gathered around their radios to hear an announcer in Honolulu describe the attack.

Everyone listened intently, but no one listened more closely than Boys Town's mayor, James Ross. His hometown was the Honolulu they were describing on the radio. The other boys fired questions at Ross, asking him for details about exotic Hawaii. That evening, Ross and twenty-five of the older boys stayed up far into the night, discussing what they should do. The next morning, they marched into Boys Town's Welfare Department and told the director, Thomas Pendergast, that they wanted to leave immediately to join the military.

Pendergast tried to talk the boys out of their decision, urging them to finish school. They were stubborn and refused to budge. The boys did agree they needed to talk to Father Edward J. Flanagan. He had no objection to his boys joining the military. In fact, their desire to serve their country made him proud. What he objected to was their desire to leave before they graduated. Father Flanagan and Brother Basil, director of

121

the Boys Town High School, cited President Roosevelt's advice for everyone to remain calm in this national emergency. They asked the boys if they thought they were doing what the president wanted them to do. The boys reluctantly agreed to wait, and returned to their classrooms and dormitories.[1]

Father Flanagan thought he had defused the situation, but he began to hear reports of some fifteen- and sixteen-year-old boys threatening to run away to enlist. He called all the boys to a meeting in the dining hall and spoke to them over the loud speaker. "The United States Army wants men," he declared, "Not babes in arms!"[2] In spite of his efforts, a handful of the older boys stubbornly insisted on leaving to join the military. Against his better judgment, Father Flanagan let them go. They would join dozens of his former boys already in the service. The war had become personal for Father Flanagan. Four of his boys were stationed at Pearl Harbor and he waited to hear news of them.

Donald Monroe, William Debbs, George Thompson and Walter C. Clark had come to Boys Town in the 1930s. Monroe enlisted in the Navy in 1939 and was stationed on the *USS Arizona*. In July 1941, he wrote to Father Flanagan. "I am now in Honolulu. It's very warm here. I saw the (motion) picture on Boys Town. We had it on our ship the *USS Arizona*. It was wonderful! I enjoyed myself. Everyone enjoyed it. All the boys on the ship ask me was Boys Town just like in the picture? I told them that was you up and down."[3]

Debbs joined the Navy in 1940 and was stationed on the *USS Oklahoma*. One of his shipmates was his old friend, George Thompson. On October 22, 1941, Thompson wrote his family a brief note. "Howdy Folks…I never felt better in my life. The only thing wrong is that is it pretty hot out here around the islands. We have been out to sea since Friday morning and it will be another week before we get back to Pearl Harbor.'

"I like it fine aboard ship, sure is a good bunch of fellows and they feed me well. I don't know for sure when we will get back to the States again. We're supposed to go to dry-dock in Bremerton for a couple of months in April. It might be longer though now that the Japs are giving us something to think about; I hope not."[4] In little more than two months, Debb's fears about the Japanese would prove well-founded.

Like Debbs, Clark had joined the Navy in 1940. He was stationed on the *USS West Virginia*. He watched the attack unfold from the deck of his ship and later wrote to Father Flanagan describing what he had seen.

"The seventh of December was a peaceful morning. The sun was just coming over the mountains. And at 7:50 a.m. death and destruction came out of the sky. Lots of the fellows were still sleeping, others working and still others getting ready to go to church. We were taken by surprise. But it didn't take long to man our battle stations. General Quarters was sounded, but by that time, we had been hit several times by heavy bombs. The ship caught fire and started blowing up. Other ships in the harbor were also hit by this time. The gun I was on didn't get many rounds out. But instead I helped fight fires and care for the wounded. I had several close friends killed and I sure hated that. But most everybody lost friends there."[5]

Father Flanagan didn't have to wait long to hear the news he had been dreading. A few weeks after the bombing of Pearl Harbor, he heard from George Thompson's mother that her son had died on the *USS Oklahoma*. Father Flanagan wrote back: "It is with a heart full of sorrow that I write extending to you my sincere sympathy in the death of your son, George, but at the same time I extend to you my heartiest congratulations – because of the pride that must be in your heart today for having brought into the world a son who paid the supreme sacrifice for his country.

"It is mothers like you, dear Mrs. Thompson, who are the real patriots of our country and we all admire that patriotism and that courage – and we are buoyed up with still greater enthusiasm to carry on in order that our Country may continue to enjoy the freedoms which the blood of our forefathers made possible for us."[6]

Thompson was the first Boys Town boy to be reported as killed in action. In April 1942, Father Flanagan received a letter from the Navy about Donald Monroe, who had been a cook aboard the *USS Arizona*.

"…Since the Japanese attack on Pearl Harbor, December 7, 1941, Donald Monroe has been carried on all of our lists as 'missing in action.' I believe that the Navy Department will soon declare all men still missing in this category as a result of the above attack 'dead.'

"I knew Donald Monroe very well as he was attached to my mess. He was a fine example of what a young American should be, and in every sense more than lived up to the very highest standards set by our Navy and our country.

"Donald Monroe was proud of Boys Town; I know that Boys Town is proud of him. If he was an example of the average boy from Boys Town, then I can easily see why our whole country is proud of Boys Town."[7]

Monroe, Debbs, Thompson and Clark were just the first of many Boys Town citizens to see combat in World War II. There would be Boys Town boys at Wake Island and Bataan, and in Italy, North Africa and France. They could be found in nearly every theatre of the war. Father Flanagan believed patriotism should be a core value of the citizens of Boys Town. The entire graduating class of 1942 walked from their graduation ceremony to the enlistment offices.

Father Flanagan saw the war as a struggle between good and evil. In a speech broadcast on Omaha's KOIL radio station, he thundered: "We are at war! Those are blunt words. But they tell the story of a peace loving nation being forced into war by an unscrupulous aggressor nation.

"Our American nation has a great responsibility facing it. Its people, true to their tradition and the tradition of all peace loving and free people must accept this responsibility just as the forefathers of our Republic faced it; just like all people who broke the chains of slavery, and fought for the principles of freedom that they and their children may enjoy rights given them by God, and not by men or rulers of nations. Our people realize that in order to retain their freedom, we must be strong – strong in mind, body and soul.

"What a catastrophe – what a tragedy. Men, women and children, created by God of love to live and love, and be rewarded in eternity for that love, must be subjected to the infamous brutality, sorrows and sufferings of war lords – dictators who have usurped the power of life and death over them…"[8]

In the first few months of 1942, the war was not going well for the Allies. The Japanese had taken Wake Island and were advancing across the Philippines. Boys Town citizens, Billy Capps and Bobby Paradise, were on Bataan. The world seemed turned upside down. However, back at Boys Town, life hadn't changed all that much. Father Flanagan wrote to Capps on April 9, 1942, to give him news from the home front.

"Everything is humming with activity here at Boys Town. I might add that I am feeling fine after my recent operation at the Mayo clinic [spinal surgery] and it sure feels good to be back on the job again.

"We are planning to have a huge Victory Garden this year. In fact, it will cover 40 acres. We hope to raise sufficient food to carry us through next winter if it is humanly possible. Of course, this will mean a lot of work, but the boys have been enthusiastic and have all volunteered to work in our Victory Gardens during the summer. I too plan to devote an hour each day to working in the garden.

"Mr. Corcoran has arranged a fine baseball schedule for our high school team this spring. We feel we have an outstanding team this year.

"I hope that you find this letter interesting. Please drop us a line at your convenience in the near future. We shall be very happy to hear from you. If you should have a photograph of yourself, please send it along, possibly we could use it in the *Boys Town Times*.

"Say your prayers and attend church regularly William. Be assured that we remember you in our daily prayers."[9]

It was a letter that Capps would never read. The day before Allied forces on Bataan surrendered, he was killed. Paradise was missing and presumed dead.

Father Flanagan heard the news from Capps' grandmother, Mary Shores Clark, several months after Billy was killed. "I wish to inform you Billy Capps, a one-time boy of yours, lost his life in action, April 8th in the Battle of Bataan," she wrote. "My health broke when I lost Billy. Please pray for him."[10]

These letters had become all too common for Father Flanagan. He wrote back to Clark expressing his sympathy. "It is with great sorrow that I read of the death of your grandson, Billy Capps, who lost his life in the battle of Bataan. He is the twentieth Boys Town boy to pay the supreme sacrifice during World War II.

"I want to extend to you, my dear Mrs. Clark, my sincere sympathy in the death of your grandson. While your heart and the heart of Billy's friends must be torn asunder because of this terrible tragedy – there still arises within you a pride that fills that great void, and I know, too, that you seek help and consolation from Him who is the great consolation of the world, and one, if we only seek His aid, will supply to us much consolation in our hour of sorrow.

"I know something about this great loss. Boys Town has lost 19 other wonderful boys and while perhaps you may think that, after all, these boys are not as close to me as they would be to a natural father, still, let me assure you, my dear Mrs. Clark, they are very close and I feel the loss of each and every one very deeply."[11]

The summer of 1942 saw the creation of a huge Victory Garden just like Father Flanagan had described to Capps. The summer's highlight was a visit by the famous comedians, Abbott and Costello, who stopped at Boys Town during a whirlwind War Bonds tour. They entertained the boys with one of their routines. A year later, they returned and donated a full set of baseball uniforms for Coach Ken Corcoran's team.

During their 1942 visit to Boys Town, Abbott and Costello also visited the backyard of a young Omaha boy who was hosting a fundraiser for the Red Cross. Father Flanagan served as master of ceremonies. Autographs of the comic duo were sold for one dollar each, but the fun really began when Father Flanagan suggested that Lou Costello auction off his shirt.

"The air was full of mosquitoes and millions of other bugs and Lou squirmed at the prospect of being shirtless. So, when someone bid $5. Lou raised him. He kept raising bids too, until his bid of $12 finally saved the shirt."[12]

In an attempt to help with the war effort, the Boys Town Scout Troop launched a scrap metal and rubber salvage campaign. The *Boys Town Times* reported, "...they have collected and forwarded to Mr. Hitler and company, 550 pounds of scrap rubber and 8,600 pounds of scrap metal."[13]

On a July trip to Washington D.C., Father Flanagan – at the request of Vice President Henry Wallace – gave the invocation at the opening of the U.S. Senate. He prayed for divine guidance in bringing about a victorious peace to the world.

"... Help us dear Lord," he said, "in this hour of peril when our nation is engaged in a war with most powerful enemies, enemies whose philosophy radically differs from ours, a philosophy which teaches that man is but a slave of the state and a helpless tool in the hands of heartless dictators. Teach us to have a deep and abiding faith in Thee, and a confidence that our great nation, built on the philosophy of man's God-given inalienable rights, shall endure as long as we align ourselves on the side of justice and rights for the common man under the leadership of Thine infallible Leadership..."[14]

It was his fierce belief in those God-given, inalienable rights and his acute sense of justice that once again placed Father Flanagan in conflict with mainstream attitudes about some of America's marginalized citizens.

The attack on Pearl Harbor set in motion powerful forces. The military machine was awakened, production plants and agricultural organizations geared up and racial prejudice reappeared.

Peter Okada, who would later work at Boys Town, recalled where he was on December 7, 1941. "I was twenty years old and living in California," Okada said. "It was a Sunday and as I was walking out of church people were talking in small groups about the attack on Pearl Harbor. I thought, where is Pearl Harbor? It seemed remote and far away. I never thought it would touch me.

"I had planned to go fishing that day and as I walked to the ocean people would stop and stare at me, then glare and curse. When I got to the coast, I could see the Army moving artillery into the tomato fields. Then I realized, 'this is serious,' and I turned around and went home."[15]

Patrick Okura, another future Boys Town employee, was on a golf course with his father-in-law on that Sunday afternoon. They endured the stares of other golfers before cutting their game short and heading home. "It was like a siege mentality," Okura recalled. "The streets were deserted and everyone stayed home with their family. That night the FBI came and raided our part of town. They picked up two thousand men, including my father, and took them to holding camps. We didn't see my father for two-and-a-half years."[16]

Sentiment against Japanese-Americans turned quickly. Some had been in the country for decades and many more were second- and third-generation American citizens. None of that mattered.

In January 1942, the campaign for the evacuation of Japanese-Americans on the West Coast began. Henry McLemore, a columnist for the *San Francisco Examiner*, was typical of many editorial opinions of the time when he wrote, "… Does the government feel the lovely California climate has changed them and that the thousands of Japanese who live in the boundaries of this state are all staunch and true Americans?

"I am for the immediate removal of every Japanese on the West Coast to a point deep in the interior. Herd 'em up, pack 'em off and give 'em the inside room at the Badlands. Let 'em be pinched, hurt, hungry and dead up against it."[17]

On February 19, 1942, President Roosevelt signed Executive Order #9066, which authorized the removal of 120,000 Japanese-Americans from California, Oregon and Washington to evacuation centers in Wyoming, Colorado and Arkansas. More than 77,000 of the evacuees were American citizens, as the government made no distinction between those Japanese born in Japan and those born in America.

Patrick's wife, Lily Okura, was the secretary for E.J. England, one of the administrators at the evacuees' temporary holding camp at California's Santa Anita race track. England was sympathetic to the plight of the evacuees and, through the Maryknoll Fathers, contacted Father Flanagan. Father Flanagan offered employment and living accommodations for up to eight Japanese families if they would come to Boys Town.

The Okuras told their friend, Katsu Okida, about Flanagan's offer and he wrote to Flanagan saying, "I know this is an opportunity for me if I can qualify for the job. Even if I cannot go, it is certainly heartening to know of someone who has taken an interest during these trying times."[18]

Father Flanagan was ahead of his time, according to Patrick Okura. "He was offering employment and living quarters for Japanese-Americans two years before the American government did. He was a man of strong convictions, and he thought what was happening to us was wrong. He was determined to do whatever he could to help."[19]

Records show there were ten Japanese-Americans working at Boys Town by the end of 1943. In all, forty-three lived and worked at Boys Town. Okura estimated that about three hundred Japanese-Americans found their way to Boys Town between 1943 and the end of the war. Most passed on to jobs and lives in other areas of the country, but they were first drawn to the area by Father Flanagan. He frequently paid for transportation to the Omaha area, provided work and a paycheck and scouted up lodging either at Boys Town or nearby.[20]

Peter Okada also found out about Boys Town from the Okuras. He was hired as a gardener and a part-time driver. He roomed with Katsu Okida, before Okida left Boys Town to join the Army, and fight and die in France with the famed 442nd Regimental Combat Team. "When I got to Boys Town, Kats was already here," Okada said. "I remember being surprised by Boys Town. I had expected high walls and bars on the windows, but it was like a college campus, peaceful and quiet. However, I did discover they had their own special rules and regulations.

"The place was governed in part by the boys. They had their own court and their own punishments. I remember hearing that one boy who broke the rules was being sentenced to the 'movie' punishment. Now going to the weekly movie was something all the boys really enjoyed so I didn't understand the sentence until I went to the show. The boy being punished had to sit with his back to the movie while everyone else got to enjoy it. It was very effective."[21]

Patrick Okura was hired as a psychologist in Boys Town's welfare department. He and his wife wanted to buy a house in the Omaha area. "I'd call and make an appointment to see the real estate agent," Okura recalled. "They were always friendly on the phone. I guess they thought I was Irish. But when they would meet me face to face they'd say, 'Oh, I'm sorry, we just sold that house.' After about the fifth time it happened, I challenged the real estate person and they said, 'Leave my office, I'm a Christian.' And I said, then why don't you act like a Christian?" With Father Flanagan's urging, Boys Town's law firm took Okura's case and in 1944 he was finally able to buy a house.[22]

In February 1943, President Roosevelt announced the formation of the 442nd Infantry Regimental Combat Team to be comprised of Japanese-Americans. Roosevelt declared that no loyal citizen of the United States should be denied the right to fight for his country. The call went out to the 110,000 Japanese-Americans in relocation camps across the country. The response was overwhelming. In Hawaii alone, more than ten thousand men applied to fill fifteen hundred slots. In the summer of 1943, Peter Okada and Katsu Okida set out to join the 442nd. Peter eventually enrolled in the Military Intelligence School in Minnesota instead, but Okida joined the 442nd, along with Patrick Okura's younger brother, Babe Okura.

Okida wrote to Father Flanagan from Italy in 1944, expressing his hope the war would soon be over. "I presume a great many of the boys have reached the age to enter the service and new ones are coming in to fill their places. I hope we can bring this fracas to an end soon so those entering the service now, need not have to go through this which we are experiencing.

"I cannot write as much as I would like, due to our own security at present. Perhaps I can write more later. One thing which I enjoy is the travel and seeing at least part of the world, which, in normal times, I would never have seen. This in itself, is very interesting, to see how the other people live.

"I find though, that all people are the same, living only in a different environment with another tongue.

"I hope you are in the best of health and that everything is alright at Boys Town. I hope we can come home soon. How I wish I could be home now. Goodbye and God Bless you Father."[23]

For Father Flanagan it was one of thousands of letters he received from his "boys" during the war. He kept up a regular correspondence with several hundred boys and heard about even more former Boys Town residents through the letters from his pen pals.

It wasn't just the boys who were leaving to join the service. Father Flanagan's nephew, Patrick Norton, who had served as his uncle's assistant for twenty-two years, joined the military and was commissioned as a captain in the Army Air Corps. Many other longtime employees also enlisted. In the face of this labor shortage, Father Flanagan struggled to keep the home operating and his boys graduating. He was also doing his part for the war effort, selling War Bonds as he traveled the country with Boys Town's outstanding football team. His War Bond tour of 1942 was credited with selling more than three million dollars in bonds.

December of 1942 marked the twenty-fifth anniversary of Boys Town's founding. Congratulations were sent from throughout the world, including one from President Roosevelt, which read: "Dear Father Flanagan, Hearty congratulations on the completion by Boys Town of twenty-five years of constructive service to American citizenship. In innumerable ways the value of your work has been demonstrated during the past twenty-five years, but in no respect more than in the splendid contribution being made by former young citizens of Boys Town now serving valiantly in the country's armed forces.

"God bless and prosper this noble work."[24]

The health problems that nagged Father Flanagan all his life were exacerbated by his relentless pace. In January of 1943, he had surgery at the Mayo Clinic to "...relieve a sciatic condition which developed from an old injury suffered years ago while playing handball."[25]

"I never felt better in my life," Father Flanagan told the boys on his return home. "My operation, which was a serious one, I have been advised, was successful and it certainly seems good to be back home."[26]

Father Flanagan had additional news that month. In January 1943, a small, fill-in-the-blanks postcard was sent to him by the Japanese Imperial Army. It was from Bobby Paradise and read: "I am interned in Taiwan. My health is usual. I am working for exercise. Please see that your health is taken care of. My love to you. Bob F. Paradise."[27] It was the first news Father Flanagan had heard from Paradise since he was declared missing and assumed killed at Bataan.

Father Flanagan immediately sent a letter to Paradise and included a copy of the *Boys Town Times*. Paradise wrote to Father Flanagan when his captors allowed. Just before Christmas of 1944, Father Flanagan received a longer note from Paradise. "I received your letters and papers from Boys Town. Last Christmas I received 107 letters from friends all over America.

"Our camp is beautifully located. We have a lovely garden and get vegetables from it regularly. We are well treated considering we are prisoners.

"I work in the hospital here and receive pay for my work each month. We have a canteen and are able to buy things available in the area of Taiwan.

"Father, I received your parcel and enjoyed it very much. I read in the prayer books each day and get many happy thoughts from them, which makes waiting for the end of the war easier. Well Father, I wish you a Merry Christmas and a glorious New Year."[28]

It was all a cruel deception. Paradise was not paid for his work in the hospital, there were no supplies available from the canteen and most of the material sent by the Red Cross was confiscated. Since being taken prisoner, Paradise had lost sixty pounds.

The Japanese had discovered that Paradise was a Boys Town boy. They used Father Flanagan's international celebrity to write letters in Paradise's name and give the world a false idea of how the Japanese were treating their prisoners of war. When the war ended, and Paradise was liberated, he was brought up on charges of treason.

"It was the propaganda letters the Japanese had written in my name that caused the trouble," Paradise said. "The government wanted to make sure I was who I said I was. They took my fingerprints and shipped them back to the States to be verified by Father Flanagan. Of course, he cleared me right away. I heard he was furious. I had no more trouble."[29]

As the war continued, the effects were being felt in cities and homes where absent fathers were not around to discipline their sons. Crime rates among youths increased due to lack of proper supervision. In an essay written for the *Boston Globe*, and later reprinted in the *Boys Town Times*, Father Flanagan lamented this neglect of the nation's boys.

"… Boys who gang up together with no other incentive than self-protection have no consideration for the rights of others, since they have had no rights of their own or at least experienced a minimum of such rights. Boys who have not been loved and protected are not likely to love others and protect the rights of others…

"… A forgotten boy knows no gratitude. Society, in his estimation, has done nothing for him… His home life has seared his very soul. Bad example has been his teacher. He has no ambition to take advantage of an education, for he has not been exposed in his environment of neglect to an inspiring element that would open his heart and mind and soul to that other kind of ambition possessed by children of more normal parentage."[30]

He continued to believe that reformatories and youth prisons were not the answer and consistently spoke out against corporal punishment. In a letter to a donor, he explained his opposition to this type of restraint.

"Personally I am opposed to physical punishment of any kind and look upon it in over 95% of the cases as administered by helpless adults who, because of their inability to solve the particular problem of discipline under discussion, lose their temper and punish, out of the natural urge of anger to get revenge. I could never see where there was any rehabilitating side to physical punishment except that which was administered by a kind and loving mother to a little child."[31]

Of course, not everyone agreed with Father Flanagan and his methods. Many considered him to be too lenient and criticized him for sheltering youths whom they believed should be in prison. A woman from Hastings, Nebraska, criticized Father Flanagan for taking in boys who had committed murder, saying they would give Boys Town a bad name. Father Flanagan was unapologetic in his reply.

"I have had murderers in my Home, something like one hundred entirely during the twenty-six years, also some bank robbers and car thieves, and others guilty of major crimes. I have been very successful in dealing with these children and restoring them to a normal state of mind after they became familiar with a different kind of teaching and training, and they learned that the world was really not as bad as they had experienced. I do not take these children for any other purpose other than to just try to save them. Unfortunately, the newspapers grab this kind of story and play it up. This is the part of a sensational press and I suppose like many other disagreeable and disconcerting matters in our social life – we have to meet these things and do the best we can under the circumstances.

"Only ten percent of our boys have ever been in any trouble, ninety percent come from broken homes or the homes of bad and neglectful parents. I do not know of any other way whereby I could save a child from a life of crime in a penitentiary other than to offer the facilities of my home. If that is going to hurt the good name of my Home – then I suppose my Home must suffer, for it will suffer for the same cause for which Christ suffered."[32]

Just a few months later, Flanagan had an opportunity to prove he meant what he had written. A young boy from Iowa, who had killed his stepfather in January of 1944, was temporarily put into Father Flanagan's custody. When the court refused to rehear the case, Flanagan was forced to return the boy to the Iowa State Penitentiary in Fort Madison, Iowa. He wrote a statement to the press saying that, in his twenty-seven years of working with troubled boys, he had never met a boy who had tried harder to rehabilitate himself. He had earlier put up a $25,000 bond because of the faith he had in the boy and he vowed to "leave no stone unturned in an effort to have him returned here."[33]

As the war drew to a close, Father Flanagan's boys in uniform often were on his mind. In a letter to a mother who had written about how she feared for the life of her son fighting overseas, Father Flanagan wrote about why he thought the war was worth fighting.

"… I read an article a few weeks ago that had been written by a young American airman. He was explaining why he was fighting. It seemed simple to him, he said and he couldn't understand why some people imagined one had to have an extraordinary spiritual insight or a Ph.D. in sociology to know why one was fighting. He said that he could stand idly by and see every painting by Rembrandt, Leonardo da Vinci and Michelangelo thrown into a bonfire and feel no more than a deep regret. But throw one small, insignificant Polish urchin on the same bonfire, and he'd pull him out, or else. He has lost his life since. He would not have been happy standing idly by. I have in the neighborhood of six hundred boys fighting to keep thousands of 'urchins' out of the hands of mad and Godless men. That is what I want them to do, and I am very proud of them.

"I pray that God will bring them back, of course, and it is perfectly true as you say that all of us, from the Pope on down, are praying mightily for peace. But the Church has never understood by 'peace' a mere absence of armed hostility, such as prevailed between the two great wars. She holds with the age-old definition of St. Augustine that peace is the tranquility of order; an ordered society, and when she prays ardently for peace, she understands perfectly well that there may be a great deal of anguish to be endured in obtaining that order, but she prays, that in the end it will be established."[34]

In August 1945, the war finally ended. Eight hundred former Boys Town citizens served in the U.S military during World War II, and forty gave their lives for their country. Father Flanagan was proclaimed the "Number One War Dad in America."[35] The last years of his life were to be spent, sometimes in joy, sometimes in anguish, helping children all over the world and trying to find that tranquility of order of which St. Augustine had written.

9

Helping the Children of Defeat

FATHER EDWARD J. FLANAGAN first met Franklin Delano Roosevelt in November 1932 when the New York governor was traveling across the country as a presidential candidate. Roosevelt and his wife, Eleanor, toured Boys Town declaring it one of the most beautiful places they had visited. It was the start of an enduring friendship between the two men.

In August 1944, Father Flanagan wrote to Roosevelt about the need for a plan to help displaced and homeless children in Europe. Flanagan foresaw the end of the war and the chaos that would ensue. As always, his first concern was for the children.

"…When the war has been won on the battlefields of Europe, there will be literally millions of orphan children left homeless, destitute and abandoned. There will be many whose fathers will not return, and whose mothers will have been the victims of atrocities, or who have perished through various other natural or unnatural causes. There will be others who will be fatherless, but whose mothers will not be able to properly provide for them.

"If these children are neglected, they will constitute a very serious problem in the immediate future and in the years to come. During adolescence, and before they reach maturity, they will be easy prey to temptation and crime, and to infection from the various noxious *isms*. It will be a long time before war-torn Europe will be able to properly care for these war orphans, and in the meantime they will endanger any permanent peace policy. If, however, they are properly cared for, trained and educated in the true traditions of their respective countries, and if they are given Christian care and love, they will become the most able leaders in the peaceful rehabilitation of their countries."[1]

Father Flanagan envisioned a three-pronged approach to dealing with the problem of war orphans. First, he would establish communities, based on the Boys Town model, that would feed, clothe, house and educate these children. The plan also would allow widowed mothers and their children to live in these communities, with the women providing whatever help they could.

Second, similar communities would be set up in neutral countries and, whenever possible, those in charge would be from the refugees' home countries so that "their education and training could be continued in the tradition of their homeland."[2]

Third, children also could be placed with individual families in neutral countries, including the United States. He concluded by writing, "… If you feel, Mr. President, that my knowledge of this problem, gained through many years of actual experiences, can be effectively applied, my humble services are yours to command at any time."[3]

Roosevelt promptly wrote back and thanked Father Flanagan for his offer, writing that, "… It is a matter, of course, which disturbs the minds of all of us that have any responsibilities for the situation in Europe after the German collapse."[4] Roosevelt continued that the major responsibility lay with the countries themselves, but that they would be unlikely to have the financial resources to deal with the problem. The United Nations Relief and Rehabilitation Administration had been created for just this challenge. Roosevelt promised to send a copy of Father Flanagan's letter to those in charge and added, "... I am sure that in developing any such plans they will wish the benefit of your experience and I will suggest to [Former New York] Governor [Herbert] Lehman that they get in touch with you.

"We all appreciate your interest and most timely suggestions."[5]

Less than a year later, on April 12, 1945, Roosevelt died of a cerebral hemorrhage in Warm Springs, Georgia. Father Flanagan's offer of assistance would not be forgotten, but it would be left to Roosevelt's successor, President Harry S. Truman, to deal with the problem of the war orphans in Europe and Asia.

While Father Flanagan was worried about the children of the world, back home in America he was concerned about racial injustice. In a letter to a Jesuit priest in Detroit, Michigan, he wrote about his attitude toward racial equality.

"... I know when the idea of a boys' home grew in my mind, I never thought of anything remarkable about taking in all of the races and all of the creeds. To me, they are all God's children. They are my brothers. They are all children of God.

"... Who am I that I should think that Christ, when he died on Calvary, died only for the Catholics living on millionaire row and white Catholics at that. My understanding of Catholic doctrine is that Christ died for the Negroes, for the Mexicans, for the Germans and for the Japanese, and for all of these other nationalities and why should I, therefore, set up a church and become a dictator as a Pastor in that church, and say that my church is exclusively for the white race and that the Negro must not worship here. That would smack of the attitude of the innkeepers when Mary and Joseph entered into the little town of Bethlehem and were greeted with the answer, 'There is no room.'

"I think one of the most remarkable and outstanding results of the gift of faith in the Negro is the fact that he has persevered in spite of the opposition he has received. He must indeed be very close to Christ and he knows something of the Cross that Christ carried. He carries it, he must know..."[6]

Living in a time and place where segregation was the law of the land and racial prejudice was not only practiced, but encouraged, Father Flanagan's philosophy was decades ahead of its time. A donor wrote to Father Flanagan objecting to the use of "colored" boys in photographs taken of Boys Town. Flanagan replied, "... I regret your attitude and that you are opposed to my philosophy – that Negro boys are endowed with hearts, minds, and souls and are children of God just the same as you and I and are our brothers, brothers in Christ. We must be more Christ-like in our attitude towards other races and creeds."[7] He used whatever means he could to show his disdain for bigotry and discrimination based on religion, nationality or race. One of the tools he used was sports.

Father Flanagan always had believed in the power of sports to help heal troubled boys. In the beginning, he had organized sandlot baseball games to provide him with some common ground with his boys. Basketball, boxing and even marble tournaments eventually joined baseball as sports enjoyed by Boys Town's citizens. But the king of the Boys Town sports was football. Originally playing with donated and mismatched equipment, the football team at Boys Town evolved into a national powerhouse. Between 1935 and 1940, the team was undefeated, with a record of 40–0.

The team played in front of crowds numbering in the thousands. In October 1944, Boys Town played Detroit Central Catholic to a 14–14 tie in front of more than 43,000 fans. Father Flanagan used these tours to promote Boys Town and, during the war years, to sell War Bonds. He received letters from Boys Town alumni from throughout the world during World War II. Most asked how the football team was faring.

Father Flanagan saw football as a way to showcase the racial equality that existed at Boys Town. In a time when many states strictly segregated their sports teams, Boys Town's football teams featured players of every race and color. Their unmatched success validated Father Flanagan's philosophy of racial equality.

In the '30s, the Boys Town teams played local teams, but in the 1940s, they played large schools throughout the country as local teams refused to schedule them. Maurice "Skip" Palrang replaced Ken Corcoran as football coach in 1943, and Boys Town's athletic teams went on to unprecedented success in the '40s and '50s.

In 1946, Boys Town's team was 10–0 and was scheduled to finish the season with a game against St. Peter and Paul Catholic High School in Miami, Florida. St. Peter and Paul also was undefeated and the champion of the Catholic league in Florida. The Hotel Blackstone, a resort hotel on Miami Beach, extended an invitation to Father Flanagan and his boys to stay there, cost-free, during the team's visit to Miami. The game was expected to draw 30,000 spectators and President Harry Truman was invited to attend.

The success of the *Boys Town* movie, and national publicity about Father Flanagan and his work with troubled boys, had made celebrities of him and his football team. The Blackstone was eager to host these celebrities until managers discovered the team included black players. It was a possibility they may never have even considered as no Florida team would have included white and black players on the same roster. In an attempt to rationalize his decision, the manager of the hotel wrote to Father Flanagan with his concerns:

"Conditions which the management of the Blackstone cannot control, mitigate against registration of Negroes. We do not subscribe to narrow-mindedness but after exploring potential reaction find that the boys would probably be subject to embarrassment. We do not care about prejudice aimed at the hotel. Our first reaction was that Negroes who in the eyes of God are welcome at the gate of Heaven should be welcome at a resort hotel, but careful consideration indicates that the holiday we wanted to give the boys would be spoiled by reaction which would make them conspicuously uncomfortable.

"If there is any revision in your plans which would by-pass this unfortunate issue please let us know."[8]

Through Byron Reed, Boys Town's director of public relations, Father Flanagan responded that he and Coach Palrang would never consider leaving behind any of their players.[9] The entire squad traveled to Miami. Boys Town, led by its African-American quarterback Tom Carodine, crushed the Florida champs, 46–6. The boys enjoyed their stay and were oblivious to what had happened leading up to the game.

Father Flanagan was proud of his record of achievement at Boys Town, not just in sports, but more important, in the successful lives of Boys Town's graduates. In February 1946, he challenged Missouri Gov. Philip Donnelly about a comment the governor had made to the press: "We have some of Father

Flanagan's graduates at Booneville [the site of Missouri's youth prison]."[10] Always ready to defend his boys and Boys Town's reputation, Father Flanagan promptly wrote a scathing reply, which he shared with the media.

In his letter to the governor, Father Flanagan admitted that there were three current residents of Booneville who had spent some time at Boys Town. However, he took issue with the governor's definition of "graduate," pointing out that one of the boys had been at Boys Town about four months and the other two had been there fifteen and six days respectively.

"... In fairness to Boys Town," Flanagan wrote, "I believe a statement from you correcting your previous statement would be in good taste. Your statement had all the earmarks of an attempt to embarrass Boys Town by citing cases of three boys whom you chose to call Boys Town graduates, but whom I emphatically deny are graduates of Boys Town. Your statement made no mention of the good being done for the seventeen Missouri boys at Boys Town today. Nor did it make mention of the good accomplished by the one-hundred boys who have come from Missouri and who have taken advantage of our facilities the past five years. Would it not have been fairer, before putting yourself out on the limb, for you to have ascertained the full details concerning these three boys, and to have informed yourself of the care that has been given to other boys from your great state? In view of the fact that you made such a statement to the press I am taking the same privilege of sending a copy of this letter to the press in your state. In the spirit of fair play, I know you would want me to do this…"[11]

With the war over, Father Flanagan's attention once again turned to how he could help more children. In a Board of Trustees meeting in January 1946, he announced that contracts had been "…let on a portion of the estimated three million dollar building expansion program…"[12]

"…The program approved more than a year ago by Father Flanagan's board of trustees, calls for the building of a new unit at Boys Town for boys of high school age. Present facilities will be used by grade school boys and will give Father Flanagan the opportunity of reducing the minimum entrance age of 12 so he can care for all boys grade school age…"[13]

The plans included construction of an administration-welfare building, a reception center, a new high school, a dining hall, a trade school and twenty-five cottages that would each house twenty boys. Construction was expected to take eighteen months to complete and, when finished, Boys Town would be able to care for five hundred boys of high school age and an additional five hundred grade-school boys. Father Flanagan hoped to break ground for the new buildings in spring 1946.

With construction soon to start at Boys Town, Father Flanagan began to prepare for a long-planned visit to Ireland. Although he wanted to see his family and tour some of his old haunts, he had an ulterior motive for the visit. For some time, he had received letters from friends and acquaintances about the conditions at Ireland's reform schools.

In a letter to his friend, the Rev. Thomas F. Collins, Father Flanagan asked Collins to put him in touch with Frank Fahy, the speaker of the Irish Parliament. He wanted to talk with Fahy to get a comprehensive picture of the Irish penal institutions for adults and juveniles. "I also want to visit these institutions," Flanagan wrote, "but I am particularly interested in the juvenile problem. I would like to get their reaction as to whether these so-called training schools conducted by the Christian Brothers are a success or a failure. My memory – and it is not very clear – has been that they have not been very successful in developing individuality, Christian character, and manliness, because they are too much institutionalized. This as you know, helps the good Brothers and makes it easier for them.

"I am wondering if the Dublin authorities might be interested in establishing a Boys Town program somewhere in Eire. Perhaps the Bishop might want something of that nature. Of course, they may not like dictation and they may not like any new ideas from outside, but I do think that we have something that will develop homeless and abandoned children along more constructive lines than what is now being accomplished. I thought I would write to Frank Fahy along this line, but in a confidential manner."[14]

With a Boys Town already established in Australia and plans being discussed for building Boys Town facilities in India and China, Father Flanagan saw Ireland as the logical place to build his first European Boys Town. In a letter to Frank Mascarenhas of Bombay, India, he talked of his June trip to Ireland and his desire to spend time studying its penal system and working with Irish authorities.

"...Most of the training schools in Eire are conducted by the Christian Brothers, and confidentially, they are not doing a very good job. They are supported by the government and they run institutions – and you can capitalize every letter of that word institutions. There is no home life, no individual training, just like our training schools in this country, with perhaps a little more religious training. I have visited some of these institutions – one of the largest at Artane, Dublin – and I left there sick at heart. I intend to make a more minute study of it on my next trip in June. I hope at that time to have an opportunity of talking with the welfare agencies and perhaps the Archbishop of Dublin. I want to show him some of the pictures of Boys Town and the basic philosophy on which Boys Town is founded, and perhaps we might get an invitation to establish a unit in Eire that might become an example, just like you are proposing to do in Bombay and would like to do also in China…"[15]

The Irish were excited about Father Flanagan's arrival. The *Irish Independent* prominently displayed a story about the anticipated arrival of Father E.J. Flanagan and his brother P.A. Flanagan. They were to be met by their sister and two nephews as well as representatives from Father Flanagan's old school of Summerhill College. The paper mentioned the Hollywood film with Spencer Tracy, but pointed out that Boys Town was flourishing long before the film. "Its story is that of one man's endeavor, of a fight against overwhelming odds, of a tenacity to overcome difficulties, of a struggle spurred on by a simple slogan that 'There is no such thing as a bad boy,' It is ultimately the story of a success."[16]

The *Irish Independent* continued its coverage once Father Flanagan arrived, laying out his schedule. "…During his month's stay in Ireland, Monsignor Flanagan hopes to visit the Christian Brothers' schools at Artane and Letterfrack. His engagements will include the opening of a Youth Week in Belfast on June 23. He will speak in the Mansion House, Dublin on June 28 and also meet the Commission on Youth Unemployment at the Department of Industry and Commerce.

"On the following Sunday he will open a fete at Castlerea and on July 7 will lecture in Cork and in Limerick. He will return to the U.S. on July 12…"

The paper continued the story with a brief outline of Father Flanagan's philosophy that children are not born bad, but are a product, for good or evil, of their environment. The paper quoted Father Flanagan on reform schools, noting his opinion that, "Reform schools have nothing to offer in the line of reform. It is detention and punishment all the time. We have not advanced in that direction since the days of Charles Dickens, who was one of the greatest reformers of his day."[17]

Typical of Father Flanagan's tour was his welcome when visiting his home town of Ballymoe. "It was a simple and joyful homecoming, appropriate too, in that hundreds of children gathered around the car that brought the founder of Boys Town from Rineanna to this peaceful Connacht town. Bonfires blazed outside Ballymoe. Scrolls bore the simple inscription, 'Welcome,' and bunting and tricolors spanned the streets. Standing outside the church where he worshipped as a boy, Msgr. Flanagan gave a message to the parents of Ireland."[18]

Father Flanagan told the assembled crowd, "It is important that we first understand our children, because by understanding them we can solve their problems. Children must be loved and where we have love we are willing to make sacrifices. God, in His infinite providence and divine mercy gave us that necessary patience in dealing with the many little difficulties that crop up in life and, above all, we must be patient with children."[19]

Throughout his Irish journey, Father Flanagan commented on the practice of institutionalizing boys who got into trouble. During a speech in Dublin, Father Flanagan said a child could not be reformed by lock and key and bars, and fear would never develop a child's character.[20] He called the Borstal system, Ireland's reform school system, "...a scandal, un-Christlike, and wrong."[21]

While in Belfast to kick off a Youth Week, Father Flanagan found time to not only speak about juvenile delinquency, but also to criticize the partition of Ireland. He described partition as a disaster. "… It saddles a small and comparatively poor country with two expensive legislatures and civil services and it tears in two an economic entity which nature obviously intended to be a unit. Worse still, it violates the elementary principle of democracy and fair play…"[22] He also took aim at English foreign policy, particularly as it pertained to Northern Ireland and the alleged persecution of Catholics there. "… And let me add that while in the U.S.A. we admire the anxiety of your great neighbor to right the wrongs of Indians, and Egyptians and Jews and Greeks and Syrians, we find it extremely difficult to understand why she overlooks the wrong at her own doorstep."

The book, *Suffer the Little Children: The Inside Story of Ireland's Industrial Schools*, includes a chapter about Father Flanagan's visit to Ireland. Father Flanagan's last stop before returning to America was July 7, 1946, in the city of Cork. "Addressing a packed house at the Savoy Cinema in Cork, he stated: 'You are the people who permit your children and the children of your communities to go to these institutions of punishment. You can do something about it, first, by keeping your children away from these institutions.' These remarks brought prolonged applause from the audience."[23]

Upon his return to America, in a statement to the press, Father Flanagan had continued his crusade:

"… My brief stay did not permit a visit to all of Ireland's penal institutions. I did visit some. In addition to this I learned of conditions from the lips of others. I was saddened to find that physical punishment is still used as an accepted form of punishment…

"… There is also the case of a fifteen-year-old lad at Glin [Glin Industrial School] who was brutally flogged. He is one of the few who have been able to escape after such beatings so that their mistreatment might be exposed. The signed statement of the doctor who examined the wheals on his back states that they 'were such as would be produced by a leather thong.'

"I also have the statement of the two educated men who had inside knowledge of the Borstal in Cork a few years ago and who assert that the boys there 'feared school which was run without imagination and where punishment was severe.' One warder at another place states they had to 'give the works' and 'a dust-up' to some boys.

"Conditions such as these will never be corrected as long as they are ignored or complacently shrugged off. The good people of Ireland can be trusted to do what Christian charity demands if they know the facts. The problem is to get the facts before them.

"… Advocates of physical punishment usually are intolerant of constructive educational methods. Kindness is considered as sentimentalism and mollycoddling. They brag of being of the old school which used 'stickology' instead of psychology. They attempt to justify physical punishment with the assertion that 'these wrongdoers brought it on themselves.'

"The weakness in this kind of thinking is that it minimizes the importance of the individual. It does not draw any line between the offense, which should be hated, and the offender, who should be loved as a precious child of God…

"… Flogging and other forms of physical punishment wound the sense of dignity which attaches to the self. The result of such negative treatment is that the boy comes to look upon society as his enemy. His urge is to fight back not to reform…

"… Avoiding facts and appealing to clichés and individual prejudices is as futile as trying to settle a dispute by seeing who can shout the loudest. Little is gained unless argument leads to inquiry. I would cause injury to no one. I would impugn no man's motives. My prayer is that the Christian people of Ireland will see the conditions as they are and that they will take such action as they themselves may choose in attacking this problem which can be solved through deep religious faith in the fatherhood of God and the brotherhood of man."[24]

Father Flanagan's remarks ignited a firestorm of protest from the Irish government. On the floor of the Irish Parliament on July 23, 1946, Minister of Justice Gerry Boland accused Father Flanagan of using "offensive and intemperate language" concerning "conditions about which he has no first-hand knowledge."[25] In a sarcastic twist on Father Flanagan's famous slogan, Boland was quoted as saying, "Father Flanagan is a bad boy."[26]

James Dillon, another political leader, said: "Monsignor Flanagan turned up in this country and went galumphing around...got his photograph taken a great many times and made a variety of speeches to tell us what a wonderful man he was and of the marvels he had achieved in the United States. He then went back to America and published a series of false-hoods and slanders."[27] Father Flanagan responded to these attacks by stating that his remarks seemed to have made people in authority in Ireland "rather uncomfortable."

The issue was fought in the Irish press for several months with the Irish taking sides. A Mr. P. O'Reilly wrote to the *Times Pictorial* on September 7, 1946: "Through original sin children are naturally vicious little savages, and it needs a rigorous discipline with fear as a wholesome deterrent to mould them into decent citizens." Another writer responded that O'Reilly was a "particularly disgusting type of prig."[28]

Father Flanagan limited his public comments on the issue,

but in private correspondence was more direct. In a letter to an Irish friend in February of 1947, he wrote, "...the institution-alization of little children, housed in great big factory-like places, where individuality has been and is being, snuffed out with no development of the personality...and where little children become a great army of child slavery in workshops, making money for the institutions which give them a little food, a little clothing, very little recreation and a doubtful education."[29]

Mary Raftery and Eoin O'Sullivan, who wrote about Ireland's industrial schools, added: "What emerges so powerfully from Fr. Flanagan's private correspondence is his overwhelming sense of outrage at the mistreatment of children in industrial schools in Ireland. All of his life he spoke out passionately against the physical punishment of children. He perceived the beating of a child as being, without exception, destructive and motivated by a combination of revenge and ignorance..."[30]

Ireland's government resisted Father Flanagan's call for reform of its industrial schools, but the priest would not give up. He was determined to make a return trip to Ireland. He wrote to the Irish government asking permission to visit a number of adult and youth penal institutions during a trip he was planning for the summer of 1948. But first, he must travel to the Far East.

In a letter to his sister Kate Staunton, he wrote about a coming trip to Asia. General Douglas MacArthur and the War Department had asked him to take a sixty-day tour of the Far East to study the problems of homeless and abandoned children. He added that an Army colonel in Germany also had written and asked for his help in setting up a Boys Town in Germany. "...Of course, there are many Boys Town Homes being established after the pattern of Boys Town and it looks as if a great deal of my time will be taken up in assisting others in this kind of work…"[31]

Father Flanagan flew across the Pacific, with stops in Honolulu, Hawaii; Guam and Manila. While in the Philippines, Father Flanagan searched for and found the grave of Billy Capps, a former Boys Town citizen killed at Bataan. From Manila, he took a transport ship north to Tokyo, where he met with MacArthur.

The pace of Father Flanagan's Asian tour was hectic. "Between April 24 and June 23, 1947, Father Flanagan visited sixteen Japanese and South Korean cities, conducting large mass public meetings in each with MacArthur and Japanese leaders. He talked with residents of forty-eight orphanages, shelters, reformatories and refugee centers.[32]

Japan always had a strong family tradition, but with the destruction of homes and the loss of many parents as war casualties, there was no established system in place to help these homeless children. "… Now children ran the streets, stealing and begging, a shock to older Japanese. Often they lived in the underground railways. With an interpreter, Father Flanagan poked into the stations nightly, talking with the children, hearing their complaints, investigating them."[33]

Father Flanagan's tour of South Korea was distressing. He believed Korea's youths had experienced no real childhood. They were expected to become wage earners at an early age. "The children do not play in Korea like the children of other countries," Father Flanagan said.[34]

Father Flanagan's report, "Children of Defeat," was presented to Truman in a private meeting on July 7, 1947. He recommended that a foster home system be created and that the American occupation forces help educate the Japanese people about this concept. He also called for tighter regulation of orphanages, "…to make racketeering impossible behind the guise of aiding helpless, starving little children.[35]

Father Flanagan returned home to sad news. While he had been away, his long time friend and ally, Henry Monsky, had died of a heart attack in New York City. An article in the *Boys Town Times* eulogized Monsky. "In his death, Boys Town has lost a staunch friend and supporter. The loss affects not only Boys Town, but the nation as well, for Mr. Monsky was a leader in the affairs of the nation and the world."[36]

Impressed by his work in Japan and Korea, President Truman asked Father Flanagan to undertake a similar fact-finding mission to Western Europe. Time and travel were taking their toll on Father Flanagan. He had suffered from ailments of the lungs all of his life, but his fierce will to help children continued to drive him to physical exhaustion. He confided to friends that he would like a rest, but he could not turn down the president. He knew there were thousands of children in Europe who needed his help. He packed his bags and, with his nephew Patrick Norton, left New York City on the *Queen Mary* on March 5, 1948. He was leaving for Europe by ship, the same way he had arrived in America, nearly forty-four years before on the *S.S. Celtic.*

Norton and Flanagan arrived in London on March 11 and departed by plane for Frankfort, Germany, the same day. From Frankfort, they traveled to Vienna, Austria, arriving the next evening. The two men stayed in Vienna for weeks, using the Bristol Hotel as their headquarters. They visited schools, hospitals, orphanages, factories and prisons. Norton made daily entries of their journey in his diary.

On Easter Sunday, March 28, Father Flanagan celebrated

a Solemn High Mass at the Blessed Trinity Church. Just after noon, as they were eating lunch, Father Flanagan collapsed while reading the newspaper. In his daily diary, Norton wrote that his uncle was "pale as death." A doctor gave Father Flanagan an injection to get blood circulating again in his arms and legs. Two days later, Father Flanagan was given an electrocardiograph to check his heart. He was advised to return to the hotel to rest for several days, eat lightly and stop smoking.[37]

On April 3, the two men took a train to Blumbach and spent several days touring the mountains, even visiting Hitler's former residence near Berchtesgaden. They traveled to Salzburg, visiting youth facilities along the way.

In a letter to Rev. Edmund Walsh back at Boys Town, Father Flanagan wrote about a trip from Innsbruck where the Russians had stepped on to the train to inspect their papers. After inspecting the papers of Colonel Nuwer, a traveling companion, the guard next checked Father Flanagan's papers. "He came into my compartment and grunted and seemed to be very dissatisfied that there was nothing wrong with my papers and then threw them on the floor instead of handing them to me. The insults are terrible, but we are advised to take no notice of these insults."[38]

On May 10, 1948, Father Flanagan and his nephew flew from Vienna to Frankfort, Germany. On May 14, they flew to Berlin. En route, one of the plane's engines failed. They flew the final seventy miles on one engine. Fire trucks and an ambulance were waiting for their arrival in preparation for an emergency landing.

While meeting with military authorities in the afternoon, Father Flanagan learned about the ten thousand homeless children in Berlin. They decided to meet again the next day.

Norton's diary contains a stark record of what would be Father Flanagan's last hours. "At midnight a knock came to my door. It was Father telling me to call a Doctor, that he had a pain in his chest. I called the Station Hospital 279, and asked them to send a Doctor immediately, and in about 15 minutes he was there."[39]

When Dr. Bartholomew Clemente arrived, he "…found a man in his sixties blue and vomiting with severe chest pain and having difficulty breathing… I gave him a shot of morphine and quickly transported him in the ambulance. I told the driver to hurry but to be careful to avoid bumps in the road. The ride was not comfortable even on the stretcher for Father Flanagan. I apologized to him, but he was gracious in that he felt better knowing he was in American hands. Once we arrived at the hospital, he was put to bed, an oxygen tent was ordered and an intravenous of glucose was started. I called the chaplain and he came quickly. Father [Emmett] Walsh, was very attentive to Father Flanagan."[40]

Following hospital protocol, Clemente notified the colonel at the hospital. "He was gruff and did not care who Father Flanagan was and never realized his significance," Clemente wrote. "The usual bigot towards anyone of Father Flanagan's religious bent, the colonel also had no love for Father Walsh. Even though at that time, I was not particularly religious, I knew what wonderful things Father Flanagan had done. When Father Walsh came, Father Flanagan asked for Extreme Unction so the two in unison said the Latin prayers for the anointing of the body and asking God for his love, care and if not healing, to be received by Him to everlasting life."[41]

A little before two in the morning, Walsh finished giving the Last Rites to Father Flanagan, intoning, "Support him with your power, comfort him with your protection, and give him the strength to fight against evil. Since you have given him a share in your own passion, help him to find hope in suffering, for you are Lord for ever and ever."[42]

With the habit of his lifetime, Father Flanagan responded with a last, whispered, "Amen."

His Work Continues

FATHER FLANAGAN KNEW he was mortal. He knew his time working with troubled youths was drawing to its end. His health had dogged him since he was a youngster living in Ballymoe to his years studying for the priesthood, to his time at Overlook Farm caring for his boys. In a conversation with his biographers the day before he sailed for Europe, Father Flanagan shared his thoughts about his home for boys – and how Boys Town would go on without him.

He talked about how efforts to secure the home's future were under way. Someday, he said, he envisioned the home being self-supporting. "Anyway, the work will continue, you see, whether I am there or not, because it is God's work, not mine."

In parting, his biographers had asked what they could do for him. Father Flanagan's reply: Say one Hail Mary for his health.[1]

Ed Novotny, a former Boys Town boy who was working at the Home, took Father Flanagan to the airport for his final, fatal journey. Father's mind was racing, Novotny recalled. Father Flanagan told Novotny and a co-worker about the many construction projects on campus: new cottages for the boys, a new music hall, a new high school, a new trade school and a new fieldhouse. He also talked about how the campus needed landscaping work. "'When I get back,'" Father told Novotny, "'I'll have to worry about paying for it.'" Finally, Father Flanagan pledged to travel to Kansas City when he returned to talk a former employee into coming back to the Home. "Father planned to sit on his stoop until he agreed to come back."[2]

Others would have to carry out those plans. Although Father Flanagan's work would continue as he had predicted, America first would mourn the loss of one of its most giving and caring citizens.

That grieving took many forms. The Rev. Peter Dunne, a Boys Town dean, was traveling with the Rt. Rev. Msgr. Francis Schmitt near Dubuque, Iowa, when they heard a radio broadcast about Father Flanagan's death. They slowed their car and pulled to the side of the two-lane highway. There, they prayed.[3]

At Boys Town, all activities quickly came to a halt, Novotny recalled. Athletic games stopped. The boys returned to their apartments. Later, the Rev. Edmond Walsh called the boys together in the gymnasium. "He told the boys what had happened and then he said, 'I think we need to go to Dowd Chapel and say some prayers.'"[4] Preparations quickly began for Father Flanagan's funeral. American flags were flown throughout campus, as they were at graduation or when a dignitary visited the home.

Although Boys Town was mourning the loss of its leader, administrators knew life must go on. Boys attended school and did their chores. Novotny recalled that the distraction helped.

Six days after his death in Berlin, Father Flanagan was laid to rest in Dowd Memorial Chapel on the Boys Town campus. An estimated fifteen hundred people, including 450 Boys Town boys, were at the airport when Father Flanagan's body arrived aboard a C-47 from Frankfurt. En route from the airport, the funeral car carrying his body stopped momentarily at Twenty-fifth and Dodge Streets to note the residence where Father Flanagan first established his first home for boys more than thirty years before. One Mass – intended for Boys Town boys, alumni and staff – drew fifteen hundred people. A second Mass – open to the public – drew twenty-five hundred. Several thousand other mourners listened to the service outside Dowd Chapel. An estimated thirty thousand people viewed Father Flanagan's body as it lay in state the two days before burial.[5]

Walsh, assistant director of Father Flanagan's Boys' Home, read from Matthew 25 during the Requiem Mass said for Father Flanagan: "For I was hungry, and you gave me to eat; I was thirsty and you gave me to drink; I was a stranger and you took me in." Those words reflected Father Flanagan's life, Walsh told his mourners: "To himself, Father Flanagan was humble, but to the world he is great, because he loved much and therefore gave much."[6]

Walsh explained how some might view May 21, 1948, as a day of grief and sorrow. Yet, the day was the final act of a story that Walsh described as thrilling, humble and very great. Walsh told of the priest's humble beginnings tending his father's sheep in Ireland. He talked about Flanagan's poor health as he studied to become a priest. "Through the years, fragile health threatened him," Walsh said. "But he refused to acknowledge such threats, even if he had to get up time and again from a sick-bed that would have forced most men to an early death or a life of inactivity."[7] Finally, Walsh recounted Father Flanagan's struggles to establish a home for boys. Although a struggle, world leaders embraced his efforts and sought his advice. Walsh then explained how Father Flanagan wouldn't refuse a request for his help.

"Even in his last moments, death had to hunt and find him amid the turmoil of Berlin. He did not want to make this trip. When he first told me of the invitation from the American Government, he told me, too, that he was afraid the trip demanded more strength than he had. But he refused to consider passing by the opportunity to serve his country."[8]

Monsignor Nicholas Wegner, Chancellor of the Omaha Archdiocese, also spoke at the Requiem Mass. Wegner spoke of Father Flanagan's devotion to his cause and to his God. "We thank God for the life and deeds of this great man, Monsignor Flanagan, whose service to his country shed an undying luster on his country, whose holiness and erudition sets his name high among American clergy; and whose love of justice and humanity inspired the noble deeds that will forever immortalize his memory."[9] Father Flanagan's last will and testament that he left to his boys and to the world, Wegner said, was a heritage of compassionate love, understanding and kindness that is found only in the sacred heart of Jesus.

Following the final services, Father Flanagan's body was placed inside a sarcophagus and sealed with a marble slab. The inscription: "Father Flanagan, Founder of Boys Town, Lover of Christ and Man."

Word spread quickly throughout the world of Father Flanagan's death. A radio broadcast the day after Flanagan's death told of how a small community in Nebraska was mourning the loss of its best friend – a legend of charity and kindness.[10] Coverage of Father Flanagan's death and burial by the newspaper wire service, United Press International, described how six Boys Town boys carried the priest's casket to the tomb. Other Boys Town boys were part of an honor guard around the casket.[11] An Indiana newspaper noted that two leaders in the American youth movement had died on the same day: Father

Flanagan and Dr. James E. West, who had been chief executive of the Boys Scouts of America for thirty-two years. "Dr. West and Father Flanagan led highly useful lives and saved many boys from blighting and destructive influences. Their work was constructive, and will live after them."[12]

Letters of condolences arrived at Boys Town soon after Father Flanagan's death. Among the messages were:

President Truman: "American youth and youth everywhere have lost an ever faithful friend in the untimely death of Father Flanagan. His unshaken confidence in the love of God and in even the least of God's children found eloquent expression in the declaration that there is no such thing as a bad boy."[13]

Kenneth Royall, secretary of the U.S. Army: "Father Flanagan has died in the service of his country and in the service of all mankind. His entire life was devoted to such service, and the world will remember him for it."[14]

Leopold Figl, federal chancellor and foreign minister of the Republic of Austria: "His memory will remain unforgettable and his name will continue to live in the history of the education and training of youth."[15]

Frank Leahy, University of Notre Dame football coach: "His marvelous influence and tremendous inspiration could not be measured and will continue to guide each of us who had the privilege of knowing him."[16]

Spencer Tracy, who portrayed Father Flanagan in the Boys Town movies: "The memory of a man as great as he was will help sustain them (Boys Town boys) in their sorrow for he was truly a fine, a good man."[17]

In a tribute that was included in the *Boys Town Times*, Rabbi Edgar Magnin of Los Angeles described how Father Flanagan embraced the scarred and the maimed without question.

"He reached out his arms, took them to his bosom. He counseled with them. Some were black. Some were white. There were Jews, Catholics, and an infinite variety of Protestants, and those who called themselves by no name and knew no God because they had never been taught there was a God until they met Father Flanagan."[18]

Hundreds of letters and cards of condolence arrived at Boys Town from friends, former boys and supporters living through the country and aboard. Many included memorials – one dollar, two dollars, sometimes even ten dollars – given in Father's name to help carry out his work. Some letters expressed sorrow that Father Flanagan died too soon. Others noted that they were Honorary Citizens of Boys Town and had supported Father's work previously. Still others marveled at his life's work, expressing optimism that his efforts would continue.

An Alabama attorney, in a letter of condolence, called Father Flanagan one of the world's most profound thinkers. The author wrote that once Father Flanagan belonged to Boys Town, but, in recent years, he belonged to the entire world where boys in need could be found.[19] Another letter came from a man who noted he was a Protestant. Father Flanagan, he wrote, was "the greatest man that ever lived."[20] A letter from the United Packinghouse Workers of America, Local 107, reported that members paid their last respects to Father Flanagan through a standing vote of thanks for his great work.[21]

A California woman wrote about meeting Father Flanagan in Yankton, South Dakota, years earlier when the Boys Town Choir had performed there. The woman promised to keep Father's last letter and card. "I am proud to be an Honorary Citizen of Boys Town."[22]

A letter from Japan arrived days after Father Flanagan's death. The writer, an Osaka woman, had been recognized by the Japanese press for her work with more than twenty children of lepers. She had been inspired by a visit from Father Flanagan during his trip to the Orient a year earlier and had decided to raise one of the children as her own. Her impressions of Father Flanagan remained vivid, she wrote. "I am always offering prayers for the baby, that it will become a good man of God like Father Flanagan."[23]

Although his humanitarian trip to Europe went unfinished, newspaper accounts following his death carried Father Flanagan's message. Before his death, Father Flanagan had praised the work of the U.S. Army in Austria and Germany, but called for more funding and more workers. He also called for a return to religion in Middle Europe. Youths in Austria and Germany must learn about God, he urged. "...[I]t is a question whether we can get the youth of the two countries to learn something about God, on whom alone real citizenship can be based. Without that, there isn't any hope. Without God, you will have other leaders with just as false philosophies as Adolf Hitler and Benito Mussolini."[24]

Father Flanagan, forever the humble priest, died with little personal wealth. A newspaper account noted that Father Flanagan, who had founded Boys Town with a borrowed ninety dollars that grew into a home for boys valued at ten million dollars, had left his estate to his sister Nellie Flanagan. "While I have accumulated very little of worldly goods, whatever estate and property, of whatsoever nature, and wheresoever situated, of which I may die seized or possessed, I hereby give..."[25] An estimate of the value of his estate, according to the newspaper account, was about one thousand dollars.[26]

Nine days after Father Flanagan's death, the Omaha Archdiocese newspaper announced that Father Edmund Walsh would serve as interim director of Boys Town. Walsh had served as assistant director of Boys Town the past two years, and had been acting director while Father Flanagan had been on his War Department mission in Europe. Monsignor Nicholas Wegner, the Omaha Archdiocese chancellor who had spoken at Flanagan's funeral, indicated that the permanent successor wouldn't be named until the Most Rev. Gerald Bergan, Omaha archbishop and president of the Boys Town Board of Trustees, returned from a trip to Australia.

Walsh noted that no one could replace Father Flanagan. He affirmed the message that Father Flanagan had shared with his biographers shortly before he left for Europe: "The work he began will be carried on as he would have wished with unfaltering fidelity through the principles and ideals his life personified."[27] Walsh noted that Father Flanagan had prepared Boys Town for moving forward without him.

After the funeral, some Boys Town boys began to worry. They worried that Boys Town would close without Father Flanagan. Some even made plans to leave, Novotny recalled.[28] Walsh reassured the boys and told them to stay put.

Father Flanagan's travels in the past decade had meant he was away from Boys Town for long periods of time. He had set up a chain of command for those times, which provided the blueprint for operating Boys Town after his death.

Four months after Father Flanagan's death, the Omaha archbishop appointed Monsignor Wegner as the permanent replacement. Wegner, who served as Boys Town's director for the next twenty-five years, paid homage to his predecessor: "Let's keep this thought in mind: The great founder of Boys Town, Msgr. Flanagan, will always live in spirit here. I will try to follow him in every way possible, to work in his footsteps. He made such a success of his work here. If I can keep in that same path, I will have some measure of success. For that I ask your prayers for me. Pray for Msgr. Flanagan that he may watch over you and watch over Boys Town."[29]

Following Monsignor Wegner, three other men – Father Robert Hupp, Father Val Peter and Father Steven Boes – have led Boys Town in turn. Each expressed gratitude to Father Flanagan for the work he began, and the work each pledged to continue.

"In 1973, when I came upon the scene, it was not a great feat to move ahead," Father Hupp said. "We see far, you know, when we stand on the shoulders of giants. It was the charismatic program innovator, Father Flanagan, complemented by the administrative executive, Monsignor Wegner, who provided the frame for me to climb."[30]

Father Peter said: "Father Flanagan's mission of changing the way America cares for her at-risk children is still our mission today. His mission is a gift to all of us (boys and girls, families, workers, donors and supporters). To carry out this mission requires an enormous effort, but the blessings are even greater."[31]

Most recently, Father Boes, during his inauguration speech in 2005, told how he had spent the previous night in Father Flanagan's house, which remains at Boys Town. "Kneeling at the foot of his bed last night, I sensed his powerful strength, the strength that fired his dreams. I sensed his energy, his commitment to children. And this morning when I woke up, on the dresser was one of his hats. I just had to try it on. It was too big. I should have known. There is really only one true leader of Boys Town, our founder, Edward J. Flanagan."[32]

As Monsignor Wegner promised, the work to help America's troubled boys continued – from the day after Father Flanagan was laid to rest, to today. The Boys Town Choir continued to receive high praise for its performances. Boys Town athletic teams continued to win many games and matches. A senior Boys Scout troop formed. Most important, more boys came to Boys Town seeking a second chance.

In December 1948, the Boys Town boys celebrated their first Christmas without Father Flanagan. Boys attended a Christmas Eve Mass or Protestant service. They spent Christmas day in their apartments or cottages – except to eat a roast turkey dinner with Wegner and to watch a Christmas movie. Under Christmas trees in each of the forty-five cottages at Boys Town was a large console radio – donated by Bing Crosby.[33]

As the decades following Father Flanagan's death passed, Boys Town expanded its continuum of care. One thing, however, remained constant: kids come first at Boys Town.

In his day, Father Flanagan relied on local physicians whenever one of his boys became ill. Those who were supportive of his cause donated their services. Boys who suffered from more serious ailments would be taken to a local hospital. Eventually, Boys Town included an infirmary. Sick boys received care from the various orders of nuns who lived and worked at Boys Town. These days, Boys Town offers a variety of primary and specialty care services. The Boys Town National Research Hospital, which has become an internationally recognized leader in treating deaf or hard-of-hearing children and children with speech disorders, opened in 1977 in Omaha. The core principles behind the hospital are that children who are deaf or hard of hearing, are visually impaired or have related communication disorders can become productive members of society. The research hospital, with two locations in Omaha, treats thousands of children each year.

Boys Town also provides foster family services, treatment foster care, intervention and assessment services and in-home family services throughout the country. The Boys Town National Hotline is a toll-free crisis and resource referral service. Trained counselors assist callers twenty-four hours a day, seven days a week.

In 1983, Boys Town admitted girls for the first time. Hupp, then director of Boys Town, explained the reason behind the change. "One of the things I really wanted to do was try our program on girls, to see if it works as well for girls as it does for boys. And I'm happy to say it does."[34]

Four years later, the first girls graduated from Boys Town High School. Five girls were among the forty-six Boys Town graduates on that day in May, 1983. Joni Bachelor, who came to Boys Town in 1980, was among the five. "I'm proud to be a Boys Town graduate because it represents togetherness. Here, all of us are the same and we don't leave anybody out. Where I went to school before, I never had that chance."[35]

Decades earlier, Father Flanagan had provided hints as to why his efforts focused solely on boys. The April 1919 edition of his *Father Flanagan's Boys' Home Journal* included an overview of the Omaha juvenile court system. Occasionally, the article explained, a hardened youngster would show up in court who asked for no sympathy from anyone. "What is said of the boys applies equally to girl delinquents that are brought before the court, only that there is likely to be more sympathy shown a girl with the least spark of redemption smouldering within her, through the efforts of the several women who interest themselves particularly in such cases."[36]

Apparently, Father Flanagan believed that boys would be treated more harshly in the court system and, accordingly, needed extra attention and special care – his attention.

Actually, a girl – a toddler – had stayed with Father Flanagan at the German-American Home in about 1918. He had received a telephone call from the mother of two boys who were staying at the home. The woman told Father Flanagan that she was leaving town and her husband – and had given her young daughter to an elderly woman who was living in a basement near Twenty-fourth and Douglas Streets. She begged Father Flanagan to care for her daughter – as he was already caring for her sons.

Father Flanagan asked the elderly woman to give him the baby. She initially refused, until Father Flanagan displayed the badge he had been given by the police department. He took the toddler with him and handed her over to one of the nuns who was assisting him at the Boys' Home. "No child was better cared for than that baby was that night."[37] The next day, a woman from rural Nebraska visited the home. She was in Omaha hoping to adopt a baby girl. The woman eventually adopted the girl.

Father Flanagan's plan was for America's troubled youths to come to Boys Town. He figured he could best care for them if they were with him, in his home. In 1987, Boys Town took Father Flanagan's dream to Florida when it opened a residential site for children in Tallahassee. More sites would follow. "We have tried to raise the level of child care so that what we do is replicable across the United States," Father Peter said. "I can say, 'Come up to Boys Town. I will train your people and they will get the same skills our people have at Boys Town.'"[38] Boys Town now offers direct care to children and families in more than a dozen states and the District of Columbia.

In a tribute to Father Flanagan shortly after his death, the *Evening World-Herald* asked a question that has been answered time and again: "How well Boys Town will do without Father Flanagan only the future can tell. Let it be hoped that his personality and Christian spirit have been so strongly imprinted upon it that it will not only live on, but grow in usefulness to America's young manhood."[39]

It has, as Father Flanagan said it would.

AFTERWORD

THE SHADOW OF FATHER FLANAGAN looms over Boys Town. It is present, not only in the chapel where his body rests, or in the sculptured reminders of his person, but in the spirit that hovers over the place. Some visitors are unaware that he has been dead for over fifty years, so real is his presence. And those for whom Boys Town is filled with memories expect to see him rounding a corner or walking from his office to the chapel, each time they visit Boys Town.

His was a varied personality. No one person could grasp that many-faceted personality, shaped by many battles, educated in a variety of roles before he found his niche. He was at once clever and simple, direct and subtle, a man of vast experience, yet childlike.

It is not so much the historical and geographical milieu in which Father Flanagan moved that reveals the man: it is the vision and conviction that guided him. That vision and conviction was a simple one: the worth of a single human being. This was the sacred law by which he lived, and it was a principle that had seared itself into his very flesh. This was evident especially in the first days of his work when he moved among those whom others regarded useless drifters and vagrants. When *he* looked at jobless drifters and social outcasts, he saw men. And he treated them as men, whatever others might think. He had no illusions about success or reform, for this was not his aim. He became their friend, and friendship sets no limits to its service.

In the living of this conviction, he was indeed rare and unique. Men of every walk of life, of varied backgrounds and faiths, saw something in him that won their devotion and esteem. Many thought him a saint. Thousands of others called him friend although they had never seen nor spoken to him. Even his critics admitted a quality they could not define. Something shone through the humanity of the man, which charmed some and irritated others; some reflection of God and Christ which burned at the very center of his being. It is that which has remained at Boys Town, still casting its shadow after these many years. To understand Boys Town, one must understand Father Flanagan.

Father Flanagan's total vision of his work found its full expression in Boys Town, in the concept of the boy, not as a ward of an institution or the inmate of a home, but as a citizen, still in a state of formation, but already possessing dignity and rights. The concept was at work early when his collaborators were pitifully few, and older boys were made responsible for younger boys, and the senior students were consulted in matters that affected the welfare of all.

His was a religious mind, but it was not loaded with pieties, and was singularly ecumenical long before the word or concept was fashionable. The Flanagan mind was tough and resilient, shot through with an unusual blend of theological and psychological insight. Upon this insight, he built, not a philosophy, but Boys Town, and his insight is embodied in several generations of boys.

His application of Christian principle to the concrete circumstances in which he moved and the moral fiber and intellectual insight he displayed were classical in the best sense of the word. The superb artistry with which he maneuvered his work for boys into the public eye and changed with a few bold strokes of imagination the passion and prejudices of a whole generation suggests something more than priestly piety and Irish wit.

Those who knew him knew the flint-like persuasiveness of his every uttered word, the hardness of his character and the depths of his feeling, his gift for friendship and his dog-like devotion to family and friends; the tongue that tripped on clichés and fed on platitudes; the gallant, uncalculating and sometimes mathematical mind; the swift, spontaneous and vigorous handshake; the insatiable appetite for work, the unperturbable confidence in the strange destiny that Providence had thrust upon him.

During his lifetime, by his style and by the magnitude of his own achievement, he created his own legend, a legend that is somehow larger than the man, and yet in some way less than the spirit and vision that guided him.

The grain of his personality was a rare blend of humanity, insight and sheer nerve, coupled with an educated innocence that had looked deep into the inescapable tragedies of the human situation and decided to do something about it. He died at mid-century having straddled three continents with his labors. He left behind an imperishable memory and an example of faith and daring that antedated the *aggiornamento* of Pope John XXIII and the monumental achievements of the Second Vatican Council.

It is a pleasure and a joy to see his life and achievement laid out as it is in the pages of this book. Millions have seen his life and work dramatized in the person of Spencer Tracy in the movie that hit box offices exactly seventy years ago, and Boys Town today is expanding Father Flanagan's work in ways that he himself only dreamed about. In a conversation with President Franklin Roosevelt when Boys Town was scarcely twenty-five years old, he envisioned a Boys Town in every state, reaching out to neglected and troubled youth across the then forty-eight states. He saw the need and knew what he had accomplished. This book is a record of his achievement and of the vision that built a Camelot of the spirit of Boys Town.

Father Clifford Stevens

NOTES

Prologue

1. Gray, L. (1944, December 29). Two sailors executed for Wayne murder, *Jackson Daily News*, p. 1.
2. Ibid.
3. Flanagan, E.J. (1944, December 13). Personal communication.
4. Flanagan, E.J. (1946, April 17). Personal communication.
5. Flanagan, E.J. (1945, January 12). Personal communication.
6. Father Flanagan confers with Bailey in sailors' case. (1944, December 28). *Clarion-Ledger*, p. 1.
7. Ibid.
8. Leemon, Joseph M. (1944, December 28). Personal communication.
9. Gray, L. (1944, December 29). Two sailors executed for Wayne murder, *Jackson Daily News*, p. 1.
10. Flanagan, E.J. (1945, January 12). Personal communication.
11. Flanagan, E.J. (1945, January 20). Personal communication.
12. Flanagan, E.J. (1945, January 12). Personal communication.

Chapter 1

1. Willets, G. (1943). *Father Flanagan of Boys Town*. Unpublished manuscript.
2. Brady, J.J. (2005). *Ballymoe: Mogha na gCrann*. Ballymoe, Ireland: St. Croans Church, p. 148.

3. Crosfield, J. (1846). *Distress in Ireland.* NLI, Ireland: Society of Friends, p. 292.
4. McCaffrey, C. (2006). *In search of Ireland's heroes.* Chicago: Ivan R. Dee, p. 175.
5. Ibid., p. 188.
6. Connolly, S.J. (Ed.) (2002). *The Oxford companion to Irish history* (2nd Ed.). Oxford, NY: Oxford University Press, p. 258.
7. Willets, G. (1943). *Father Flanagan of Boys Town.* Unpublished manuscript.
8. Ibid.
9. Brady, J.J. (2001, May 22). *A sense of Ballymoe in 2004.* Speech, Ballymoe, Ireland.
10. Ibid.
11. Willets, G. (1943). *Father Flanagan of Boys Town.* Unpublished manuscript.
12. Ibid.
13. Ibid.
14. Brady, J.J. (2001, May 22). *A sense of Ballymoe in 2004,* Speech, Ballymoe, Ireland.
15. Willets, G. (1943). *Father Flanagan of Boys Town.* Unpublished manuscript.
16. Flanagan, Edward J. (1942, April 26). Personal communication.
17. Willets, G. (1943). *Father Flanagan of Boys Town.* Unpublished manuscript.
18. Ibid.
19. Brady, J.J. (2001, May 22). *A sense of Ballymoe in 2004,* Speech, Ballymoe, Ireland.
20. Gilbert, W. (1946). *Summerhill Annual.* Summerhill, Ireland: Summerhill College.
21. Ibid.
22. Oursler, F. and Oursler, W. (1949). *Father Flanagan of Boys*

Town. Garden City, NY: Doubleday & Company, p. 38.

23. Summerhill College. (1903, June 25). *The Sligo Champion,* p. 3.

Chapter 2

1. Weissmann, J. (1904, April 10). The landlord as czar: pre-World War I tenant activity, *New York Herald,* p.1. In www.tenant.net/ community/history/hist01.html Retrieved January 8, 2008.

2. Mount St. Mary's College. (1905). Personal communication.

3. Mulry, Thomas M. (1906, June 27). Personal communication.

4. Myham, Thomas. (1906, July 1). Personal communication.

5. Flynn, Denis. (1906, June 26). Personal communication.

6. Archdiocese of New York. Mission statement. http://www. archny.org/seminary/st-josephs-seminary-dunwoodie/mission-statement/ Retrieved December 12, 2007.

7. Oursler, F. and Oursler, W. (1949). *Father Flanagan of Boys Town.* Garden City, NY: Doubleday & Company, p. 45.

8. Coreth, Emerich, (1989, April 25). Personal communication.

9. Willets, G. (1943). *Father Flanagan of Boys Town.* Unpublished manuscript.

10. Ibid.

11. Ibid.

12. Oursler, F. and Oursler, W. (1949). *Father Flanagan of Boys Town.* Garden City, NY: Doubleday & Company, p. 86.

13. Ibid.

14. Tornado kills 60, injures 152 in Omaha. (1913, March 24). *Omaha World-Herald,* p. 1.

15. Reilly, H., and Reilly, R.T. (2003). *Historic Omaha.* San Antonia, TX: Historical Publishing Network, p. 49.

16. Oursler, F. and Oursler, W. (1949). *Father Flanagan of Boys Town.* Garden City, NY: Doubleday & Company, p. 88.

Chapter 3

1. Burlington Hotel for workingman's home. (1915, December 8). *Omaha World-Herald, 51*(59) p. 11.

2. Needs of the Workingmen's Home. (1916, February 25). *The True Voice, 15*(8), p. 8.

3. Willets, G. (1943). *Father Flanagan of Boys Town.* Unpublished manuscript.

4. What the home accomplished in 1917. (1918, February). *Father Flanagan's Boys' Home Journal, 1*(1), 4.

5. Willets, G. (1943). *Father Flanagan of Boys Town.* Unpublished manuscript.

6. Chase Jr., Francis. (1938). *The Story of Boys Town.* Unpublished manuscript.

7. 25 years of service is rewarded by a glorious record of remarkable achievements and successes. (1937, July). *Father Flanagan's Boys' Home Journal, 21*(7), p. 7.

8. Ibid.

9. Willets, G. (1943). *Father Flanagan of Boys Town.* Unpublished manuscript.

Chapter 4

1. Willets, G. (1943). *Father Flanagan of Boys Town.* Unpublished manuscript.

2. Ibid.

3. The weather. (1917, December 12). *Omaha World-Herald, 53*(63), p.1.

4. Oursler, F. and Oursler, W. (1949). *Father Flanagan of Boys Town.* Garden City, NY: Doubleday & Company, p. 148.

5. Ibid.

6. Ibid., p. 149.

7. Ibid., p. 151.

8. Ibid., p. 154.

9. Boys Home. (1918, February). *Father Flanagan's Boys' Home Journal,* 1(1) p. 3.

10. Ibid.

11. The boy whom nobody wants. (1918, March) *Father Flanagan's Boys' Home Journal,* 1(2), 2.

12. The ladies organization of the Boys' Home. (1918, February). *Father Flanagan's Boys' Home Journal,* 1(1), 2.

13. U.S. Department of Labor. (1928). Children in street work (Publication No. 183), p.175.

14. Ibid., p. 179.

15. Ibid., p. 180.

16. Ibid.

17. Ibid.

18. The first number of the 'Boys' Home Journal.' (1918, March). *Father Flanagan's Boys' Home Journal,* 1(2), p. 12.

19. Second annual entertainment (1918, March). *Father Flanagan's Boys' Home Journal,* 1(2), p. 2.

20. Willets, G. (1943). *Father Flanagan of Boys Town.* Unpublished manuscript.

21. Ibid.

22. Ibid.

23. Financial need of the home. (1918, August). *Father Flanagan's Boys' Home Journal,* 1(6), 2.

24. Our needs. (1918, September). *Father Flanagan's Boys' Home Journal,* 1(7), 2.

25. Ban on gathering because of influenza. (1918, October 18). *Omaha World-Herald, 54*(16) p. 1.

26. Kohn, G. C. (1995). *Encyclopedia of plague and pestilence,* Facts On File Inc.: New York, NY, p. 305.

27. Total cases of flu in Nebraska is 14,092. (1918, October 18). *Omaha World-Herald, 54* (16) p. 1.

28. Kohn, G. C. (1995). *Encyclopedia of plague and pestilence,* Facts On File Inc.: New York, NY, p. 305.

29. Christmas greetings. (1918, December). *Father Flanagan's Boys' Home Journal,* 1(11), p. 2.

30. Willets, G. (1943). *Father Flanagan of Boys Town.* Unpublished manuscript.

31. Proposed farm home. (1919, February). *Father Flanagan's Boys' Home Journal,* 2(2), p. 2.

32. Our new home. (1919, October). *Father Flanagan's Boys' Home Journal,* 2(10), p. 2.

33. Willets, G. (1943). *Father Flanagan of Boys Town.* Unpublished manuscript.

34. Oursler, F. and Oursler, W. (1949). *Father Flanagan of Boys Town.* Garden City, NY: Doubleday & Company, pp. 168-169.

35. Our traveling troupe. (1920, July). *Father Flanagan's Boys' Home Journal,* 3(7), p. 2.

36. Oursler, F. and Oursler, W. (1949). *Father Flanagan of Boys Town.* Garden City, NY: Doubleday & Company, p. 170.

37. *Father Flanagan's Boys' Home Journal.* (1921, September). 3(9), p. 11.

38. The home's problem. (1921, May). *Father Flanagan's Boys' Home Journal,* 4(5), p. 3.

39. Overlook Farm. (1921, June). *Father Flanagan's Boys' Home Journal,* 4(6), p. 3.

40. We move to Overlook Farm. (1921, November). *Father Flanagan's Boys' Home Journal,* 4(8), p. 3.

Chapter 5

1. We move to Overlook Farm. (November 1921). *Father Flanagan's Boys' Home Journal,* 4(8), p. 3.

2. Witcofski, A. (1988). Oral history, Boys Town, Nebraska, p. 15.

3. *Father Flanagan's Boys' Home Journal.* (October, 1921). 4(7), p. 3.

4. $300,000 drive for Boys' Home to start July 19. (1921, July 8). *Omaha Daily Bee, 51*(18), p. 5.

5. *Father Flanagan's Boys' Home Journal.* (1920, March). *3*(3), p. 2.

6. *Father Flanagan's Boys' Home Journal.* (1919, October). *2*(10), p. 2.

7. Oursler, F. and Oursler, W. (1949). *Father Flanagan of Boys Town.* Garden City, NY: Doubleday & Company, p. 197.

8. Oursler, F. and Oursler, W. (1949). *Father Flanagan of Boys Town.* Garden City, NY: Doubleday & Company, p. 201.

9. Flanagan Home drive starts this morning. (1921, November 14). *Omaha World-Herald, 57*(35), p. 2.

10. Ibid.

11. Oursler, F. and Oursler, W. (1949). *Father Flanagan of Boys Town.* Garden City, NY: Doubleday & Company, pp. 202-203.

12. Ibid., p. 203.

13. Reilly, H., and Reilly, R.T. (2003). *Historic Omaha.* San Antonio, TX: Historical Publishing Network, p. 51.

14. Mr. Dan Desdunes instructor of our band. (1922, April). *Father Flanagan's Boys' Home Journal, 5*(1), p. 5.

15. Ibid.

16. Father Flanagan's boys' shows take to the road. (June, 1922). *Father Flanagan's Boys' Home Journal, 5*(3), p. 6.

17 .Ibid., p. 7

18. Flakes, O. (1988). Oral history, Boys Town, Nebraska, p. 10.

19. Ibid.

20. Ibid.

21. Ibid., p. 21.

22. Weisberger, B.A. (1992, April). When white hoods were in flower, *American Heritage, 43*(2), p. 18.

23. African American migration, NebraskaStudies.org, (http://www.nebraskastudies.org/0700/stories/0701_0131.html), retrieved January 12, 2008.

24. Norton, P. (1974). Oral history, Boys Town, Nebraska, p. 3.
25. Oursler, F. and Oursler, W. (1949). *Father Flanagan of Boys Town.* Garden City, NY: Doubleday & Company, p. 208.
26. Norton, P. (1974). Oral history, Boys Town, Nebraska, p. 2.
27. Entertainments. (1923, March). *Father Flanagan's Boys' Home Journal, 6*(12), p. 10.
28. Witcofski, A. (1988). Oral history, Boys Town, Nebraska, p. 18.
29. Christmas at Overlook. (1924, February). *Father Flanagan's Boys' Home Journal, 7*(11), p. 7.
30. Our record. (1925, April). *Father Flanagan's Boys' Home Journal, 9*(1), p. 13.
31. My page. (1926, January). *Father Flanagan's Boys' Home Journal, 10*(10), p. 2.
32. Ibid.
33. Boys in Knights of Honor to manage home. (1926, February). *Father Flanagan's Boys' Home Journal, 10*(11), p. 4.
34. Willets, G. (1943). *Father Flanagan of Boys Town.* Unpublished manuscript.
35. Boys in Knights of Honor to manage home. (1926, February). *Father Flanagan's Boys' Home Journal, 10*(11), p. 4.
36. Ibid., p. 4.

Chapter 6

1. Mother's Day speech. (1926, May 9). Boys Town, NE.
2. Ibid.
3. Our mortgage indebtedness. (1926, August). *Father Flanagan's Boys' Home Journal, 11*(5), p. 2.
4. Twenty-one boys admitted to home last month. (1926, December). *Father Flanagan's Boys' Home Journal, 11*(9), p. 4.
5. Our mortgage campaign. (1927, February). *Father Flanagan's Boys' Home Journal, 12*(2), p. 2.
6. Home's friends decrease mortgage from $103,200 to $30,000. (1927, May). *Father Flanagan's Boys' Home Journal, 12*(5), p. 3.

7. Sixty-five homeless boys in colleges and high schools. (1927, July). *Father Flanagan's Boys' Home Journal, 12*(7), p. 3.

8. Normal care and institutional care. (1927, December) *Father Flanagan's Boys' Home Journal, 12*(12), pp. 7, 11.

9. Ibid.

10. Babe Ruth and Lou Gehrig visit Father Flanagan's Boys' Home. (1927, November). *Father Flanagan's Boys' Home Journal, 12*(10), p. 3.

11. Father Flanagan's Boys' Home has tenth birthday. (1927, December). *Father Flanagan's Boys' Home Journal, 12*(12), p. 5.

12. Gloom Killer broadcasts for 25,000 members. (1929, March). *Father Flanagan's Boys' Home Journal, 13*(3), p. 3.

13. Willets, G. (1943). *Father Flanagan of Boys Town.* Unpublished manuscript.

14. Father Flanagan appeals to governor of Missouri for two boys. (1928, January). *Father Flanagan's Boys' Home Journal, 13*(1), p. 3.

15. Ibid.

16. Ibid.

17. Father E.J. Flanagan continues fight for release of 'Kid Bandits.' (1928, February). *Father Flanagan's Boys' Home Journal, 13*(2), p. 3.

18. Ibid.

19. Radio appeal wins release of two Shetron boys. (1928, July). *Father Flanagan's Boys' Home Journal, 12*(7), p. 7.

20. Ivey, J. (2000). *Boys Town: The constant spirit.* Chicago, IL: Arcadia Publishing, p. 33.

21. Willets, G. (1943). *Father Flanagan of Boys Town.* Unpublished manuscript.

22. Ibid.

23. Board of directors plan large building campaign. (1929, July). *Father Flanagan's Boys' Home Journal, 13*(7), p. 3.

24. Willets, G. (1943). *Father Flanagan of Boys Town.* Unpublished manuscript.

25. Boys eager to play on new ball field. (1930, January). *Father Flanagan's Boys' Home Journal, 14*(1), p. 3.

26. Willets, G. (1943). *Father Flanagan of Boys Town.* Unpublished manuscript.

27. Homes or jails. (1930, February). *Father Flanagan's Boys' Home Journal, 14*(2). p. 3.

28. Ibid.

29. Fire destroys three buildings at home. (1930, April). *Father Flanagan's Boys' Home Journal, 14*(4), pp. 2, 9.

30. Was brother of Father E.J. Flanagan, and second tenor of the famous Father Flanagan's celebrity quartet. (1930, July). *Father Flanagan's Boys' Home Journal, 14*(7), p.7.

31. Ibid.

32. Annual report shows 742 applied in 1930. (1931, July). *Father Flanagan's Boys' Home Journal, 15*(7), p. 5.

33. Willets, G. (1943). *Father Flanagan of Boys Town.* Unpublished manuscript.

34. Ibid.

35. Ibid.

36. Ibid.

37. Ibid.

38. Ibid.

39. The quest for parole for the unfortunate Hubert Niccols in Walla Walla. (1931, November). *Father Flanagan's Boys' Home Journal. 15*(12), p. 8.

40. Willets, G. (1943). *Father Flanagan of Boys Town.* Unpublished manuscript.

41. Ibid.

42. An open letter to Father E.J. Flanagan. (1932, January). *Father Flanagan's Boys' Home Journal,16*(1), p. 3.

43. Two little boys walk from Missouri to find home with Father Flanagan. (1932, July). *Father Flanagan's Boys' Home Journal, 16*(7), p. 5.